FAMILY ADVENTURE GUIDE™

UTAH

"The Family Adventure Guide series . . . enables parents to turn family travel into an exploration."
—Alexandra Kennedy, Editor, *FamilyFun* magazine

FAMILY ADVENTURE GUIDE™ SERIES

UTAH

FAMILY ADVENTURE GUIDE™

by
MARGARET SANDBERG GODFREY

A VOYAGER BOOK

The Globe Pequot Press

OLD SAYBROOK, CONNECTICUT

Copyright © 1997 by The Globe Pequot Press, Inc.

All rights reserved. No part of this book may be reproduced or transmitted in any form by any means, electronic or mechanical, including photocopying and recording, or by any information storage and retrieval system, except as may be expressly permiitted by the 1976 Copyright Act or by the publisher. Requests for permission should be made in writing to The Globe Pequot Press, P.O. Box 833, Old Saybrook, Connecticut 06475

Family Adventure Guide is a trademark of The Globe Pequot Press, Inc.

Library of Congress Cataloging-in-Publication Data is available.
ISBN 1-56440-870-1

Manufactured in the United States of America
First Edition/First Printing

To Louis and Nora,
life's best traveling companions

UTAH

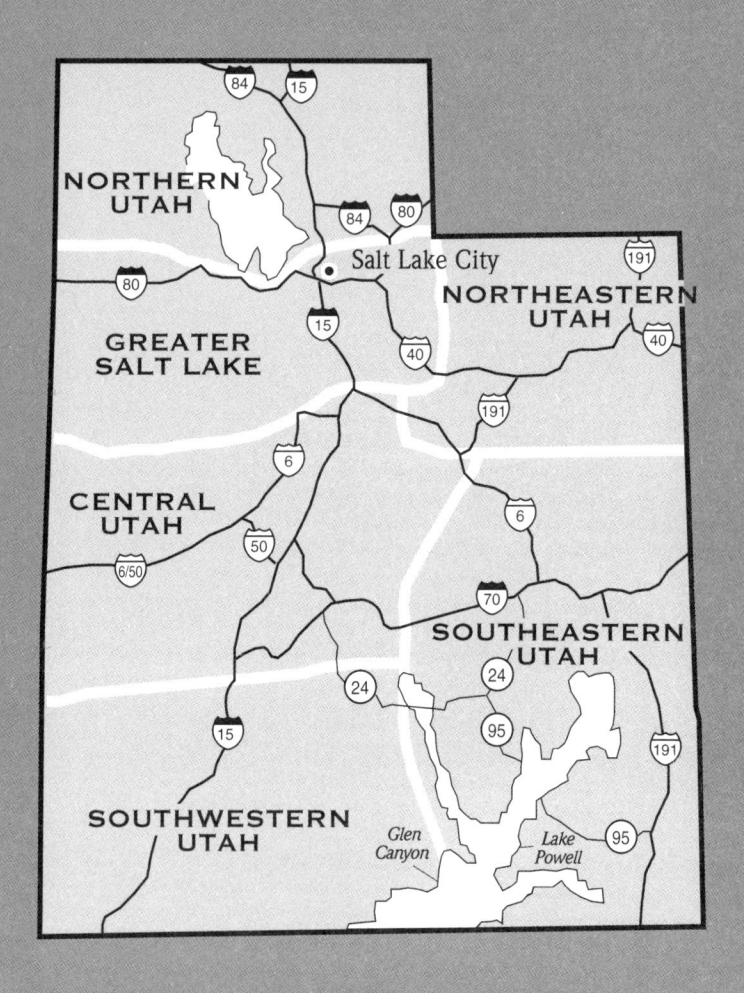

CONTENTS

Introduction, ix

Northern Utah
- 1 -

Greater Salt Lake
- 27 -

Central Utah
- 55 -

Northeastern Utah
- 87 -

Southeastern Utah
- 99 -

Southwestern Utah
- 125 -

General Index, 146

Activities Index, 157

INTRODUCTION

In Utah we're lucky and we know it. The 84,990 square miles of our state are filled with natural wonders so dense and disparate that a lifetime is not enough to explore them all. We have dozens of mountain ranges, including one that appears to float above the ground, another that beats a mysterious underground noise, one that we like to call the steepest range in the world, and the westernmost peaks of the Rockies, which provide water for most of our population. We have vast a desert crowded with psychedelic twists of red and gold rock and another paved with white salt that sparkles as far as the eye can see. We have a million acres of farmland and a million more where horses, sheep, and cattle graze. We have snowfed mountain lakes that the hottest summer sun can't warm and an inland sea that creates its own weather. We have tortoises and shrimp and cacti that are found nowhere outside our borders. No matter how many trails we hike or back roads we explore or flowers we identify, we Utahns know that there are always more wonders just around the next bend, waiting for our discovery.

Our indoor entertainment is just as varied as our out-of-doors recreation. The history and wildlife museums that proliferate here are the result of a people with a passion for documentation and a legacy of unique histories. The caliber and quantity of dance, music, and art organizations in Utah are a surprise to visitors. We support the arts with an enthusiasm not found in many larger and more urban settings. Not surprisingly, Utah's big cities offer thousands of fun and educational activities. But small towns hold some of the best secrets——Helper,

Panguitch, Boulder, and Sprindale are just a few that have excellent theaters and museums waiting to be discovered.

It should be noted that Utahns are zealous about their mid-July holiday, and an unsuspecting visitor who wanders into the state on July 24 might well wonder what is going on. The first Mormons entered the Salt Lake Valley on this day in 1847, and it has become the official sate holiday, eclipsing statehood day, and some would say even Christmas. Weeks of celebration precede the actual holiday; rodeos, pageants, parades, and craft fairs abound. The wealth of events are too numerous to mention in the text of this book, but a call to any local city office will produce specific information.

A few words of caution: even experienced Utahns sometimes become victims of unpredictable elements in this part of the world. The hottest summer day can turn into a freezing summer night, and a beautiful winter day might be hiding a storm behind the next bend. The happiest travelers will be prepared. Summer hikers in Utah, especially in the southern part of the state, are advised to carry snacks and water—a gallon of water per person, per day.

Our family has traveled far and wide, and we agree that the best vacations are those close to home. We believe that the most interesting, exhilarating, fun, and yes, weird, times we've had have been in our own backyard. We wish you the happiest of travels.

> For this guide considerable effort has been made to provide the most accurate information available at the time of publication, but readers are advised always to check ahead, since prices, seasonal openings and closings, and other travel-related factors do change over time. Neither the author nor the publisher can be held responsible for the experiences of readers while traveling.

Northern Utah

This chapter covers the busy urban area just north of Salt Lake City and then continues a trail through less-populated farming and ranching communities to Utah's northern and northeastern borders.

Some of the major recreation areas of the Great Salt Lake are here, and the wildlife-watching opportunities created by the salty lake marshes are unparalleled. Farther north, your family will find many of Utah's best-loved outdoor alpine adventure sites, including three ski resorts.

Look for Utah's premier amusement park as well as a frontier settlement that re-creates the mountain-man era. Northern Utah's dozens of museums hold collections ranging from Egyptian mummies to rocket engines. Read on to learn about other unique attractions: a park that commemorates a transcontinental railroad, the spot for famous ice cream cones, and one of the largest free-roaming buffalo herds in the world.

BOUNTIFUL

An adventurous drive that offers one of the best bird's-eye views of the Great Salt Lake is the **Skyline Drive** from Bountiful to Farmington. There are many picnic and nature walk sites along the way. The Drive is not fully paved, and parts of it may require a four-wheel-drive vehicle. Even then, it is drivable only from May through October. Ask locally for road conditions before starting out. In winter, your family will enjoy cross-country skiing and snowmobiling on this route. The Drive is accessed near the Mormon

Northern Utah

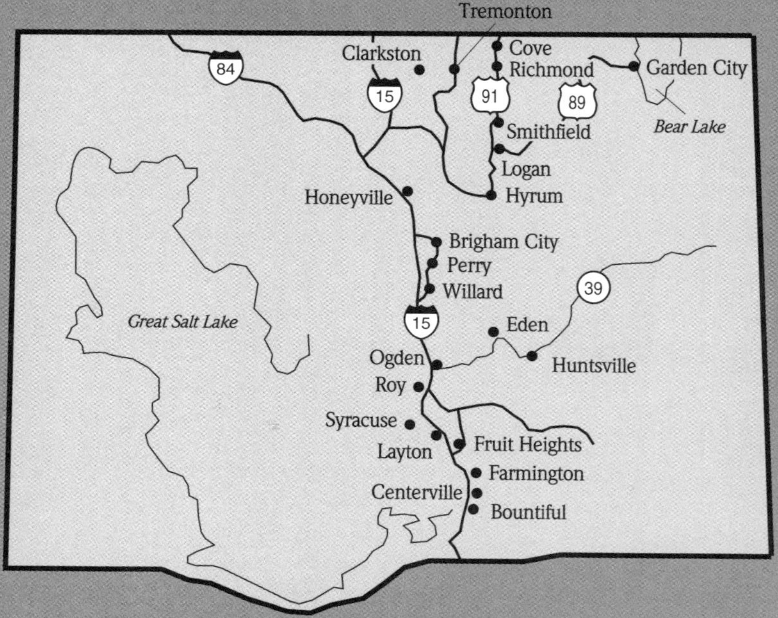

Bountiful Temple at 640 South Bountiful Boulevard. The temple grounds are open to the public.

The **Bountiful-Davis Art Center**, at 2175 South Main Street, features traveling exhibits of national artists. It is open Monday from 5:00 to 9:00 P.M., Tuesday through Friday 10:00 A.M. to 6:00 P.M., and Saturday 2:00 to 5:00 P.M. Admission is free. Each August the Art Center hosts **Summerfest**, in the Bountiful City Park at 400 North 200 West. The festival features international dance, ethnic foods, crafts, and a children's art yard. Call (801) 292-0367 for more information.

The **Bountiful Recreation Center** at 150 West 600 North is a popular year-round destination for families who enjoy exercising together. A swimming pool is bubbled in winter and open to the skies in summer. Public swimming hours vary; call for times. Young ice skaters perform leaps and twirls on the huge rink here. Again, public skating times vary. Cost for each of these activities is $2.50 for adults and about $2.00 for children. Skate rental is an additional $1.00. Call (801) 298-6220 for more information.

CENTERVILLE

The **Pages Lane Theater**, at (surprise) 292 East Pages Lane, is very popular with families for its tradition of wholesome dramas and musicals, performed live at 7:30 P.M. on selected week nights and every Friday and Saturday. Special children's plays are performed on some Saturday afternoons. Ticket prices vary, but are approximately $7.00 for adults and $6.00 for children. Call (801) 298-1302 for ticket information and reservations.

FARMINGTON

If there is a premiere "groovy kid place" in Utah, **Lagoon Amusement Park** just might be it. For more than fifty years Lagoon has offered Utahns good times and big thrills. It ranks with the best of other big city amusement parks in terms of pleasant surroundings, beautiful gardens, and, of course, exciting rides. Featured heart stoppers include the looped Fire Dragon roller coaster, the 150-foot drop Sky Coaster, and the new Top Eliminator Dragster, where riders can simulate a race down a four-lane strip and reach speeds up to 75 mph in 2.8 seconds. Three other roller coasters and dozens more rides are also part of the fun. An entire section of the park is set aside for smaller children, with pint-sized rides that move at a gentle pace. Food stands and carnival games line the walkways, along with an unending array of souvenirs to buy. Strolling singers and regularly scheduled grandstand acts provide entertainment, along with "Summer Rhythm" stage shows. An all-day pass (about $20.00) provides admission to the park as well as **Lagoon-A-Beach,** one of Utah's largest water parks, and **Pioneer Village,** a re-created Western town that features Wild West shoot-em-ups and other excitement. A 200-site campground is open early spring to late fall; call (800) 748–5246, ext. 3100 for reservations. Find Lagoon by taking the Lagoon Drive exit (327) from Interstate 15, at the junction of U.S. Highway 89. The park is open daily Memorial Day through Labor Day and weekends mid-April through September. Call (801) 451–8000 for more information.

The **Utah Botanical Gardens,** at 1817 North Main, showcase the flora of northern Utah. Ongoing experiments in plant development are conducted by Utah State University students, and visitors are welcome to enjoy the fruits of their research any day of the year during daylight hours. Tours are given each Wednesday at 10:00 A.M., May through September. Call (801) 451–3204 for more information.

The **Farmington Bay Waterfowl Management Area** is one of the places along the Great Salt Lake shoreline set aside especially for birds. Your children will love this wonderfully tranquil place, alive with pelicans, cranes, herons, grebes, and eagles. Signs in the area identify the birds and explain the surrounding geology. Bring binoculars, and find this bird-watching mecca by following Glover Lane to 1325 West Glover Lane. There is no admission fee, and the area is open daily from 8:00 A.M. to 5:00 P.M. Call (801) 451–3395 for more information.

FRUIT HEIGHTS

Right in the middle of this small town is a fun getaway: **Cherry Hill Campground** is an authentic fruit-farm-cum-destination-resort, nestled just off U.S. Highway 89 at its junction with State Highway 273. You'll find miniature "adventure golf," a wild water park, batting cages, game rooms, a swimming pool, and picnic pavilions here . . . and yes, camping, in one of

250 shaded campsites. Young children will love "hamster haven," and your whole family will enjoy the summertime outdoor theater. Cherry Hill is open daily from early spring to late fall. Call (801) 451–5379 for information and reservations.

LAYTON

If you're in need of a summer cool-off, the **Layton Surf and Swim**'s Wild Wave just might fill the bill. In summer a public pool supplies calm water, while the adjacent Wild Wave provides the thrills. In winter, one of the pools is enclosed and remains open for swimmers. Surf and Swim is located at 465 North 275 East. Call (801) 546–8588 for more information.

The **Layton Heritage Museum**, 403 North Wasatch Drive, is an interesting stop for history buffs in your family. It features collections of late-nineteenth- and early-twentieth-century items. The museum is open Wednesday through Sunday 1:00 to 5:00 P.M. Call (801) 546–3524 for more information.

SYRACUSE

Antelope Island State Park is the only place of its kind in all the world. This 28,000-acre island lies regally in the middle of Great Salt Lake and acts as a refuge for millions of shore birds on their way to and from points north and south. Other wildlife have found a home here as well, including bobcat, mule deer, coyote, and antelope. A herd of 600 bison roam the island, offering your family a first-rate view of these rare animals in a natural setting. An annual **Buffalo Round-Up** is open to the public every fall. Your family can experience real ranch action when the animals are herded by cowboys to a central area and given an assembly line vet check-up. Wildlife watching may be the best reason to visit the island, but sun lovers also enjoy the excellent white-sand beaches here. **Bridger Beach** has cabanas, picnic tables, and showers for day visitors and a primitive campground for overnighters. White Rock Bay offers a primitive camping area for groups. Antelope Island also has hiking, biking, and horse trails. Take a drive on the island's road system and stake out your own secluded spot for stunning sunsets and sunrises over the salty water; the view from any place on the island is beautiful and unique. Part of the fun of a trip to this park is

A day at the beaches of Antelope Island will please the entire family.
(Courtesy Utah Travel Council)

getting there. The island is connected to the shore by a 7-mile narrow causeway, and once you leave land you will experience a flying sensation as you become entirely surrounded by water. Biking the causeway is especially fun for older children. Antelope Island is reached by taking exit 335 from Interstate 15 and following State Highway 108 for 7 miles. There is an entry fee of $6.00 per car and $2.50 for walk-ins, bikers, and in-line skaters. The campgrounds are open during the warm-weather months; the camping fee is $8.00 per night. Call (801) 773–2941 for information and reservations.

ROY

The **Hill Aerospace Museum** is well worth a visit, and its collection of antique planes, missiles, and helicopters will captivate your entire family. The museum is devoted to the history of our national air power, and its "exhibits" are displayed in a huge indoor hangar and outdoor airfield. Self-guided walking tours will give your family a close-up view of famous war planes, including the SR-71 *Blackbird,* the B-17 *Flying Fortress,* and the P-51D *Mustang.* A restored World War II chapel and barracks are also on site. The museum is reached by following the signs from Interstate 15 exit 341. It is open Tuesday through Friday 9:00 A.M. to 4:30 P.M. and weekends 9:00 A.M. to 5:30 P.M. Admission is free. Call (801) 777–6818 for more information.

Another museum in Roy interprets the less recent past. The **Roy Historical Museum** is housed in a log cabin, and its large collection of pioneer artifacts is designed to both impress and amuse your children. The museum is just north of the Hill Aerospace Museum, on the same frontage road. It is open Tuesday through Sunday from 10:00 A.M. to 5:00 P.M. Admission is free. Call (801) 776–3626 for more information.

OGDEN

This is one of Utah's "big three" cities, along with Salt Lake City and Provo, that comprise the anchors for the Wasatch Front population. The Wasatch Mountains rim these cities, and their "front" side catches the water vital in this high desert country. Ogden's earliest recorded events were gatherings of mountain men—the rugged, pelt-covered hunters who trapped and traded fur animals. By the mid-1800s, word had spread about this valley, central to many mountain-man haunts, and several "off-seasons" were spent here. In wintertime, it seems, mountain men grouped together, "took Indian wives," and settled down in makeshift housing for several months of tanning hides, playing games of skill, and generally resting up. Ogden is named after one of these men, Peter Skene Ogden, and this valley, now called Weber County, was once called Ogden's Hole.

The first Anglo settler was Miles Goodyear, who in 1846 planted a garden, built a cabin and shelter for his animals, and constructed some outbuildings to house his mountain-man compatriots. His settlement has been re-created on its original site, and set aside as a landmark—**Fort Buenaventura State Park,** at 2450 A Avenue. The settlement has been painstakingly reconstructed from archaeological research. You'll find no modern shortcuts to construction here—wooden pegs serve as nails, and tenons lash together wooden joints. The actual number and placement of cabins and outbuildings is just as Goodyear planned it. Expect to be greeted by guides dressed in 1840s dress. Mountain men will explain what life was like back when this spot was surrounded by wilderness. Artifacts from the era are displayed and interpreted. Try to time your visit around a "rendezvous" celebration, when modern-day mountain men gather here, setting up tents, spinning yarns, playing games, and showing off the skills that were vital to "real" mountain men. The park is open daily from 8:00 A.M. to dusk; a $3.00 admission fee per car is charged. Camping at this park is available at group sites only, with a $100.00 minimum charge. Call (801) 621–4808 for information, (800) 322–3770 for day use and group camp reservations.

Goodyear's actual cabin has been moved from its original site to Ogden's **Mormon Temple Square**, and is part of the **Daughters of the Utah Pioneers Museum**. The museum is located at 2148 Grant Avenue, and is open Monday through Saturday during the summer months, from 10:00 A.M. to 5:00 P.M. Call (801) 393–4460 for more information.

In the last quarter of the nineteenth century, with the coming of the railroad, Ogden's population grew dramatically both in size and diversity. The valley proved an ideal junction as a connector for western cities in all directions. The railroad brought stockyards and industry as well as jobs and money to the area. An architectural tribute to the era remains at **Union Station**, an imposing building located in the center of town at 2501 Wall Avenue. Until late 1996 Union Station operated as a train depot. Now it is home to a wonderfully eclectic mix of museums and shops chronicling Ogden's past. Several of these are dedicated to railroading: The **Utah State Railroad Museum** is here as well as the **Wattis-Dumke Model Railroad Museum** and the **Eccles Railroad Center**. In these collections you will see an exact model replica of the 1,776-mile transcontinental route, and the largest historic railroad display in the world, featuring an outdoor pavilion that covers a 6916 Centennial locomotive, a diesel locomotive, several cabooses, and more. The **Browning-Kimball Classic Car Museum** is a collection of classic and antique automobiles from the 1930s. John M. Browning made a fortune in the firearms business, and his legacy is exhibited in the **Browning Firearms Museum** here. You'll see both original and production models of the world-famous firearms. The **Myra Powell Art Gallery,** the **Natural History Museum,** and a reproduction of an authentic Japanese tea room round out the family of museums at Union Station. They are open Monday through Saturday from 10:00 A.M. to 5:00 P.M.; during summer the hours include Sundays from 11:00 A.M. to 3:00 P.M. There is a fee for admission of $2.00 to the museums. Call (801) 629–8444 for more information.

A few steps east of Union Station is yet another celebration of Ogden's past, the shops and restaurants of **Historic 25th Street**. A hundred years ago this street was notorious for its bars and brothels, but today its restored buildings house antique stores, boutiques, and restaurants that will delight the shoppers in your family. If your children enjoy renovated architecture, take time to visit **Peery's Egyptian Theater** at 2415 Washington Boulevard. The ceiling here is "atmospheric," and during performances the sun "rises" and "sets" across its width. To arrange a tour, call (800) 337–2690.

During hot weather, a favorite family spot is **Fun City USA Water Slide Park** at 1750 South 1350 West. Besides the usual swimming facilities you will find a float-along river and a "double-trouble" slide. Call (801) 627–3525 for ticket prices.

Summer or winter, the indoor **Ice Sheet,** located at 4390 Harrison Boulevard on the campus of **Weber State University,** offers open skating to visitors on its Olympic-sized ice arena. This arena has been built as one of the venues when Utah hosts the winter Olympics in 2002. Skate rentals are available. Call (801) 399–8750 for hours and rates.

The university campus has several other family-friendly attractions. The **Layton/Ott Planetarium** in the Lind Lecture Hall opens to the public every Wednesday night, with star shows on a variety of subjects starting at 6:30 and 7:30 P.M. Weather permitting, there is a star party at 8:30 P.M. The planetarium is open September through May, and admission is $2.00 for adults and $1.00 for students and children. Call (801) 626–7907 for more information. Just a few steps away in the same building is **The Museum of Natural History**, with exhibits ranging from prehistoric animals to a display on open-heart surgery. Call (801) 626–6653 for more information. The **Collett Art Gallery**, on campus at 3750 Harrison Boulevard, features traveling exhibitions of contemporary art. It is open Monday through Thursday from 8:30 A.M. to 10:00 P.M. and Friday from 8:30 A.M. to 4:00 P.M. For information on the Collett Gallery and other visual arts activities on campus, call (801) 626–6455.

A museum dedicated to the art of learning to read is located in Ogden's City Mall. **Treehouse Children's Museum** features an Alphabet Area, a giant mechanical "Grandma" who never tires of reading stories, a Pen and Ink Studio where books and stationery are waiting to be created, and a Computer Garden. A giant treehouse forms the hub of the museum and is the stage for a regularly scheduled "partici-play," where children read all of the parts. Ongoing craft activities are based on children's books. Treehouse is a very popular place for families, especially on the weekends, so expect to wait in line for a few minutes. Admission is $1.00 for adults and $2.00 for children (you read correctly, the lower admission for adults encourages a healthy ratio), and hours are 10:00 A.M. to 6:00 P.M. Tuesday through Thursday, with later hours on weekends. The museum is open limited hours on Monday and is closed on Sunday.

Each November Ogden begins its Christmas celebration with the lighting of **Christmas Village**. The city's Municipal Park transforms into a special animated town, made merry with music and thousands of tiny lights. Call (801) 629–8214 for more information. If you visit Ogden during January you are in luck. One of the larger German festivals in the state is held at Union Station during the **Ogden-Hof Winter Carnival**. The festival is a celebration of Ogden's sister city, Hof, Germany. You'll experience German music, food, costumes, and a "ski hill" in the middle of town, perfect for small children. Call (801) 629–8242 for dates and special event information.

Ogden may be one of the few industrial cities anywhere with a wildlife sanctuary set aside in its midst. The 127-acre **Ogden Nature Center** at 966 West 12th Street sits placidly between a major Internal Revenue Service processing center and the Ogden Defense Depot, a huge storage space for military equipment. For the last twenty years the goal here has been to refurbish this land to its natural condition, as a home for wildlife replete with ponds, marshes, and thousands of trees. It features a petting farm, nature trails, picnic areas, and a museum. A "treehouse" tethered from a series of rope swings is great fun for older children. Getting out and walking the 1½ miles of nature trails is the best way to view the wildlife. Expect to see a plentitude of birds including great blue herons and flocks of regal snowy egrets. These are also wonderful trails for cross-country skiing during the winter months. Admission is $1.00 per person, $5.00 per family. Hours are 10:00 A.M. to 4:00 P.M., six days a week. Tours of the Nature Center are available for a small additional fee. Call (801) 621–7595 for information and picnic reservations.

Wildlife of a much more ancient sort can be viewed at the **George S. Eccles Dinosaur Park**, located at 1544 East Park Boulevard. More than one hundred life-size, anatomically correct dinosaur models lurk along the leafy pathways here, perched in trees and hiding behind foliage. These models reflect the very latest in dinosaur theories, and many of them are brightly colored in neon, illustrating new skin and hide discoveries. One hundred and sixty-five million years of evolution are on display here, from sluggy crawling creatures to marine life and flying reptiles. Dinosaur-lovers will relish the gorier exhibits, including a baryonyx gnashing a bloodied ancient fish. A welcome center has interpretive exhibits and a gift shop. The park is open March through November at 10:00 A.M. Monday through Saturday and noon on Sunday. Closing time changes with the season. Admission is $3.50 for adults and $1.50 for children. Call (801) 393–3466 for more information.

The Dinosaur Park is just one of a series of outdoor venues located along the **Ogden River Parkway**, 3 miles of paved paths set aside for walking, biking, picnicking, and fishing. The parkway stretches through the heart of Ogden from Washington Boulevard to the mouth of Ogden Canyon, and connects parks, gardens, and sports facilities. The last weekend of August brings families to the **Ogden River Parkway Festival** for games, crafts, music, food, and fun. Call (801) 629–8242 for event information.

Ogden Canyon follows the path of the Ogden River and squeezes out just barely enough room for a two-lane road. It is an exceptionally rugged and beautiful surround and can be a hair-raising drive for the uninitiated. Many summer homes are located here, as well as dozens of national forest campsites. For campsite information call the ranger station at (801) 625–5306. A favorite canyon outing for enthusiastic hikers is called **Indian Trail**. Consider taking two cars for this trip, and parking one at the 22nd Street terminus and then driving up the canyon to the Smokey Bear sign where the eastern end of the trail originates. Indian Trail is 5 miles long, and if you picnic along the way it will take three to four hours to complete. You will climb up and down about 1,500 feet in elevation and experience several thrilling views, some narrow-squeeze spots, low overhangs, and rock stairs along the way.

At the canyon's summit, you can't miss **Pineview Reservoir,** a favorite summer recreation area. Anchored by Pineview Dam, the reservoir reaches back in tentacle formation, about 4 miles in several directions. Fishing, boating, windsurfing, and waterskiing are popular here, and the Wasatch-Cache National Forest has supplied the reservoir with boat ramps and camping and picnicking facilities. The **Ogden Bay Waterfowl Management Area's North Arm Viewing Site** is located just adjacent to the reservoir, with excellent bird watching from its own nature trail.

Ogden Canyon leads to three ski resorts. **Snowbasin** is one of the oldest resorts in the nation, with a chair lift in operation since 1946. Its steeper slopes have been selected as the site for the downhill and super G races of the 2002 Olympic games. There are plenty of tamer runs as well inside the resort's 1,800 acres of trails. A ski school is open seven days a week during the winter, as well as a full-service ski shop and day lodge. For ticket prices and other information, call (801) 399–1135. **Powder Mountain** is another fine ski resort, with four mountain lodges, an overnight facility called Columbine Inn, and two full-service ski shops. Sixteen hundred acres of packed and powder skiing can be reached from chairlifts, and another 1,200 acres are available through snow cat skiing. Snow cat skiing involves riding a specially designed machine up the side of a mountain. Snowboarding, especially popular with teenagers, is encouraged on Powder Mountain's "half pipe" run. For lift ticket prices and more information, call (801) 745–3772. **Nordic Valley** is a favorite choice for beginner skiers, with its gentler slopes and lower lift prices. It is open seven days a week for day skiing, and Monday through Saturday for night skiing, snow permitting. Call (801) 745–3511 for information and ski conditions.

HUNTSVILLE

It's not often in Mormon country that you run across a Trappist Monastery —so if you pass by here be sure to stop in for a visit. Local people frequent the **Huntsville Trappist Monastery**, at 1250 South 950 East, for the fabulous honey collected and sold by the monks. The raspberry honey is a favorite but there are many flavors from which to choose. Eggs and bread are also sold here, in the small building just off the parking lot that the monks have set aside for temporal matters. These monks belong to the Order of the Cistercians of the Strict Observance, also known as Trappists. They dress in plain, hooded robes, and they observe a quiet and meditative life. The reception room and church are open to the public, and visitors are invited to attend services. For more information, call (801) 745–3784.

EDEN

Your family will enjoy the solitude of the surrounding hills and valleys on a guided trail ride in this beautiful area. **Carvers Cove** offers rides, by reservation, from Memorial Day through August. Call (801) 745–3018 for rates and information.

WILLARD

Willard Bay State Park's easy access from the freeway makes it an extremely popular spot for boaters, anglers, and water skiers. There are two points of entry to this 10,000-acre reservoir and marina: north (Interstate 15 exit 360), which has the best swimming beaches; and south (Interstate 15 exit 354), which is used mostly by day boaters. Here you'll find a picnic area, camping sites, restrooms, hot showers, and dump stations for RVs. If you look at a map, you might think that Willard Bay is part of the Great Salt Lake, but it is actually a river-fed freshwater reservoir, separated from the lake by a dam. Part of the park has been set aside as a waterfowl management area, and in the spring and fall it is an excellent place to watch migrating birds. For park information, including day-use fees and camping reservations, call (801) 734–9494.

A very satisfying afternoon's outing is a drive through northern Utah's **Fruitway**. This is actually U.S. Highway 89/91, a back road between the towns of Willard and Brigham City nicknamed for the fruit stands that line its path. Starting with the first harvest of summer, several dozen local growers set up shop and sell cherries, peaches, corn, peppers, tomatoes, and other fresh goods. In autumn, your children will love the weird gourds and squashes they'll find in huge supply here, including pumpkins that range in size from half-pounders to barely-fits-in-the-back-of-the-car. For about $10.00 you can amass a sizeable pile of great stuff to eat. For seasonal information, call the Ogden Convention and Visitors Bureau at (801) 627–8288.

Before you leave town, take time to look at Willard's lovely collection of **old stone houses**, which are spread over a dozen-block area. A nineteen-year-old stonemason from Wales began construction of these homes in 1862 and continued building them for twenty years. The houses are still occupied and comprise one of Utah's more unique National Historic Districts.

PERRY

Maddox, one of Utah's most-loved restaurants, is located along the rural roadside, at 1900 South Highway 89. For fifty years Westerners have trekked here for the house specialty—burgers and steaks. Call (801) 723–8545 for more information. A favorite local outing is dinner at Maddox and then a short trip down the road to **Heritage Community Theater** at 2502 South Highway 89, which offers family-oriented plays. Call (801) 723–8392 for a schedule and ticket prices.

BRIGHAM CITY

About 130 years ago the United States was in the midst of railroad fever, with Congress paying huge subsidies for those who would help connect the rails between the East and West coasts. Two companies, the Union Pacific and the Central Pacific, became the main contenders for that money, with one working its way west and the other east and each laying rail as fast as it could. The railroads finally met, on May 10, 1869, and the entire nation celebrated its first transcontinental railroad. The unlikely spot for this joining was an isolated town called Promontory, and a golden spike was driven into the last tie to mark the celebration. Promontory is now known as **Golden Spike National Historic Site**, and a visitor center's exhibits and films interpret the area's railroad history. Two working replicas of 1869 steam trains operate during the warm-weather months. Each May 10th, your family can watch the **re-enactment of the driving of the golden spike**, complete with actors in period costume. An annual **Railroader's Festival** is held the second Saturday in August. Golden Spike is found 32 miles west of Brigham City by following the signs on State Highway 83, and is open daily from 8:00 A.M. to 6:00 P.M. May through September and 8:00 A.M. to 4:30 P.M. October through April. An entrance fee of $4.00 per vehicle or $2.00 per person is charged. Call (801) 471-2209 for more information.

Two miles (and a hundred years, as they say locally) north of Golden Spike is **Thiokol Rocket Display**, an outdoor park of sorts, which houses real examples of the solid rocket motors that propel our astronauts into space. There is no charge for getting up close and personal with these huge machines. Part of the high-tech Thiokol plant, where these rockets are made, can be seen from the display area. Occasionally the rockets are tested here, and their flights can be viewed from the road. By continuing north on Faust Valley Road, you will reach another unique area called **Marble Park**. Horse-drawn wagons and equipment from the 1800s are displayed here in truly original style. Entrance to this park is also free. Call the Box Elder County Chamber of Commerce at (801) 723-3931 for more information.

If your trip to Golden Spike didn't quench your thirst for railroad knowledge, visit the old **Union Pacific Museum** in the middle of town, at

> **MARGARET'S TOP FAMILY ADVENTURES IN NORTHERN UTAH**
>
> 1. Lagoon
> 2. Antelope Island
> 3. Hill Aerospace Museum
> 4. George S. Eccles Dinosaur Park
> 5. Logan Canyon hikes

833 West Forest Street. Here you will find an educational center and gift shop documenting the history of this former major shipping center. Hours are 1:00 to 6:00 P.M., Tuesday through Saturday. There is no charge for admission. Call (801) 723–2989 for more information.

By now you have probably noticed the city's landmark, the Mormon **Tabernacle** on 251 South Main Street. Brigham City is justifiably proud of this neo-Gothic structure, with its sixteen buttresses and towers. Original construction of the tabernacle was completed in 1890, but within a decade it had burnt down and been rebuilt. Tours of the tabernacle are available from May through September during daylight hours. Call (801) 723–5376 for information.

One of the best wildlife watching areas in the state is the **Bear River Migratory Bird Refuge,** 15 miles west of Brigham City. This is the largest of the eight wildlife refuges maintained on the Great Salt Lake. The Bear River enters the Great Salt Lake here, and the resulting 65,000 acres of delta, marshes, and wetlands support an incredible variety of birds. About sixty species nest here, and many more visit on their way to and from seasonal homes. Migrating birds by the millions stop here in late summer and tank up on brine flies before heading on to their destinations. Bring your binoculars and bird guide, and drive or bike the 12-mile dike road for the best views of white-faced ibis, whistling swans, great blue herons, bald and golden eagles, hawks, and many species of ducks. The refuge is open year-round during daylight hours. Call (801) 723–5887 for more information.

If you are in town in September, you are in luck. The weekend after Labor Day, Brigham City honors its most famous crop with **Peach Days.** This is the oldest continuing harvest festival in Utah and is celebrated with a parade, antique car show, Dutch oven cook-off, and a carnival. For more information call (801) 723–3931.

HONEYVILLE

Naturally warm mineral waters make **Crystal Hot Springs Resort** a favorite family place to relax and enjoy the beauty of the surrounding mountains. Hot and cold springs supply water for six pools and three saunas, all outdoors, which are enjoyed year-round. Crystal Hot Springs is open every day except Thanksgiving and Christmas. There is a campground here, and snacks are sold at the concession stand. Call (801) 547–0777 for more information.

TREMONTON

If anyone in your family is interested in antique modes of transportation, it is worth your while to travel to 8790 West Highway 102 in this small town. Here you will find **Eli Anderson's Wagons,** one man's collection of horse-drawn vehicles—reported to be the largest private grouping in the West. Showings are by appointment only: Call ahead at (801) 854–3760.

PLYMOUTH

Another resort blessed with natural springs of warm mineral water is **Belmont Hot Springs**, found 2 miles south of this farming town on State Highway 13. Here your family can swim, golf, picnic, camp, and reportedly even scuba dive in the middle of winter. Tropical fish and lobsters are raised here in 95° water. Call (801) 458–3200 for more information.

HYRUM

If your family simply can't satisfy its hunger for elk knowledge, you'll want to visit this lovely farming community. **Hardware Ranch** exists as a year-round refuge for these beautiful beasts, and visitors here can learn about elk management and view up to 700 elk in their natural surroundings. In winter, a horse-drawn sleigh conveys passengers through the areas where the elk are fed winter wheat; the site of these animals close-up is awe-inspiring. The sleigh rides take about twenty minutes, and they are scheduled throughout the day, seven days a week, from mid-December to mid-March. Cost is $3.00 per person, with children under four riding free. A rugged backway road continues on from Hardware Ranch for 25 miles, to meet up with Logan Canyon just before its summit. This is a beautiful ride for the adventurous and informed traveler. In winter it is passable by snowmobile only, and in warm weather it should be attempted only in a high clearance vehicle. Ask locally for directions and road conditions. Snowmobile rentals, fuel, and hot meals are available near the Hardware Ranch visitor center. Find Hardware Ranch by following State Road 101 east of Hyrum for 17 miles. Call (801) 753–6168 for more information.

A small reservoir right in the middle of town is a popular local hangout for water recreation. **Hyrum State Park**, at 405 West 300 South, has a boat dock, camping facilities, and a swimming area. The reservoir is fishable all year long. Camping, day-use, and entrance fees are charged year-round. Call (801) 245–6866 for more information.

The **Hyrum City Museum**, at 83 West Main, is home to an eclectic collection of old stuff. Egyptian mummy masks are displayed near an 1872 schoolroom, and 180-million-year-old dinosaur bones from central Utah share museum space with a classic doll collection. There is truly something of interest here for every member of your family. The museum is open Tuesday and Thursday from 3:00 to 6:00 P.M. and Saturday from 2:00 to 5:00 P.M. Admission is free. The museum shares building space with the city library. For more information call the library at (801) 245–6411.

LOGAN

Cache Valley is located in the far northern reaches of Utah, where it enjoys one of the most spectacular settings of any region in the state. Surrounded on all sides by steep, forested mountains, its flat valley is criss-crossed by abundant water, large farms, and a number of small industries. Notable is the mountain range that rims the western edge of the valley. **The Wellsvilles** are said to be the steepest mountain range in the world, rising from such a narrow base. Box Elder Peak is the highest point in this range, measuring 9,372 feet in elevation. Logan is Cache Valley's largest city and an educational and cultural magnet for surrounding communities.

You might want to start your visit here with a trip to the **Chamber of Commerce Building and Information Center** at 160 North Main. Dozens of brochures are available, explaining everything from historic home tours to area snowmobile trails. Be sure to walk down the hall to the small **Daughters of the Utah Pioneers Museum**. It features demonstrations of old crafts, such as spinning and tatting, and also displays pioneer artifacts. The museum is open 11:00 A.M. to 4:00 P.M. Monday through Saturday in the summer, and occasional hours during other months. Call (801) 752–2161 for more information.

Logan's entire **Center Street** has been designated a National Historic District. As you walk past the carefully restored exteriors of these downtown buildings, it is not hard to imagine life in a bustling 1890s Western town. One of these restorations is the **Ellen Eccles Theater,** where musicals, theater, and ballet are performed throughout the year. Stop in at the **Bluebird Cafe** and order a sarsaparilla while sitting at the fifty-year-old soda fountain. Each June the beautiful Mormon Tabernacle between Center Street and 100 North is the scene for the three-day **Summerfest,** a festival devoted to music and art. The Children's Fair and Art Yard at Summerfest features hands-on giant sculpture projects, puppet theater, face painting, and special design classes. Your children will also enjoy the carnival rides and carriage trips around the tabernacle grounds as well as the food and art booths and continuous live music. For specific dates and more information, call (801) 752–2161.

Sherwood Hills Resort, 12 miles southwest of town in Sardine Canyon, is a full-service getaway. It produces outdoor theatricals in the summer, which are especially popular with children. Guided one- or two-hour horseback rides and hayrides are also available here. Call (801) 245–5054 for more information.

A child-sized zoo is found at **Willow Park,** 400 West 700 South. Take a picnic along to this beautiful area, which is dwarfed by huge trees and surrounded by burbling streams. Admission is free, but visitors are encouraged to donate 25 cents. The zoo is open 9:00 A.M. to dusk, year-round. For more information call (801) 750–9893.

The campus of **Utah State University** sits directly below the mouth of Logan Canyon, on Logan's eastern border. The school was established in 1888 as Utah's land grant college, and it has become one of the premier research universities in the United States. Free, informal tours of the campus are given each weekday at 10:30 A.M. and 2:30 P.M. during the school year and at 1:00 P.M. during the summer. To take a tour, just show up in the lobby of the University Inn at the appropriate time, or call (801) 797–1129 for details. In your travels around campus look for the Science and Engineering Research Building (called SER on campus) and find Room 132 for the **Discovery Center,** a hands-on science exploration center for children and their parents. The center is not open very often, but if your children are lovers of science this is a place worth investigating. Hours are Saturday from 1:00 to 4:00 P.M. and Monday from 7:00 to 9:00 P.M. Admission is free. A fine art museum on campus has six exhibition spaces, with rotating exhibits: The **Nora Eccles Harrison Museum of Art** features photographs, ceramic exhibits, and Native American artifacts. It is open Tuesday through Sunday. Call (801) 797–0163 for hours and information on traveling exhibits. Throw any thoughts of a fat-free afternoon away, and take your family to the **Food Science Building** at the eastern end of campus. The extraordinary ice cream sold here is made on campus by students, and it is revered world-wide for its extra creaminess.

The university operates an historical farm on Highway 89, just south of town, that makes for a fun and educational afternoon. The **Ronald V. Jensen Living Historical Farm** is preserved as an authentic 1917 dairy farm. Visitors can wander freely all over the acreage, and see draft horses, cows, pigs, chickens, and a flock of sheep "at work." Antique farm equipment surrounds the country farmhouse, barn, and smokehouse. Most weekends bring special events to the farm, including threshing, quilting, sheep shearing, taffy making, and apple harvesting. An old-fashioned Christmas is celebrated each December. The farm is open Tuesday through Saturday during the summer. Admission is $4.00 for adults and $1.00 for children. Call (801) 245–4064 for an event schedule.

Summertime on campus brings a major event known as **The Festival of the American West.** For nine days a massive 1870s-era Great West Fair encamps on the lawns, complete with mountain-man tepees, a frontier military barracks, an Indian village, a pioneer Main Street, and more. Visitors are invited to experience this history lesson up close, and watch contests of skill, quilt making, Dutch oven cook-offs, medicine shows, and old-fashioned artisans at work. A nightly mega-pageant, "The West: America's Odyssey," celebrates the settlement of the West through dance, drama, music, and multimedia effects. Tickets for the fair are $9.50 for adults and $5.50 for children; pageant tickets are $12.50 for adults, $8.00 for children. Call (800) 225–FEST for more information.

Logan Canyon, accessed directly from the eastern edge of town on U.S. Highway 89, is often named in national publications as one of the most beautiful scenic drives anywhere. Its forested walls are especially stunning in the fall, when the aspens and maples are at their height of color. The twisting, steep-sided canyon hides dozens of **Wasatch-Cache National Forest** service campgrounds. Call the Logan Ranger District at (801) 755–3620 for conditions and reservation information. There are many terrific family hikes in this 40-mile-long canyon. A level 1.5-mile hike that even very small people will enjoy is the Riverside Nature Trail to **Spring Hollow,** reached from a marked trailhead, about 5.3 miles up the canyon from Logan at Guinavah-Malibu Campground. This is a beautiful, much-photographed area, and you will see fossils of sea plants and animals along the way. A more difficult hike is found close by: A 1.3-mile steep climb will take your family 1,000 feet up to the **Wind Caves**, an exciting place that shows off rock arches and rooms formed by wind and ice. The Wind Cave trailhead is found across from the Guinavah-Malibu Campground. Adventurous older children will be rewarded with the sight of a 3,000-year-old tree if they tackle the 9-mile round-trip **Jardine Juniper Trail**. Though it's steep in places most children can hike the trail; its

Relive the days of the Old West at Logan's annual Festival of the American West.
(Courtesy Utah Travel Council)

length, however, may be prohibitive. The Jardine Juniper is 44 feet high and has a 26-foot circumference. Photographers love this tree, both for its age and its beautiful shape. The trailhead begins at the Wood Camp turn-off. A much easier hike to see another old tree is **Limber Pine Nature Trail,** an outstanding trail about 35 miles from Logan. A 1-mile loop trail takes you up through wooded paths to a huge limber pine tree, once thought to be 2,000 years old, but now discovered as several old limber pines that creatively intertwined to look like one ancient tree. The hike features plentiful wildflowers and wonderful viewpoints. A perfect place for a picnic is found 20 miles up the canyon at **Tony Grove Lake,** which is reached from a well-marked, paved road. A boardwalk leads to picnic tables near the parking lot, or take the ½-mile walk around to the Beach Area for more picnic sites.

A family-sized resort, **Beaver Mountain Ski Area,** 27 miles east of Logan, is a wonderful place for children to learn to ski. Three chair lifts and a day lodge operate here seven days a week, late November through the second week of April (except Christmas) from 9:00 A.M. to 4:00 P.M. Call (801) 753-0921 for more information. The flat, open area at the entrance of Beaver Mountain is called **Sink Hollow,** and a groomed, beginner cross-country ski trail is maintained here. The surrounding area is also popular for sledding. About a half-mile east of Beaver Mountain Resort, **Beaver Creek Lodge** offers full overnight accommodations, as well as guided horseback riding in summer and snowmobile rentals in winter. Call (801) 753-1076 for more information.

Just after you have passed the canyon summit, you will come over a rise and suddenly a panorama will be spread before you. Take time to pull off at the **Bear Lake Overlook,** with its sweeping view of the lake and beyond. You are perched on the northeastern tip of Utah, and if it is a clear day, straight ahead of you, past the lake, you can see Wyoming. To the north, at the lake's end, is Idaho.

GARDEN CITY

This tiny town is located at the spot where Logan Canyon empties onto the shores of Bear Lake. Most people who live here operate farms in the area, and their friendliness and rural pace is a welcome change from city life. Garden City's high elevation encourages cool nights year-round, providing a serendipitous climate for raspberries. You can't help but notice Garden City's pride in its star crop, as **fruit stands and raspberry shake outlets** line the roads. Raspberries are further honored with a three-day celebration the first weekend of August. **Raspberry Days** features a parade, rodeo, craft fair, and dance.

The town also supports a water recreation business for **Bear Lake,** known for its unique turquoise color. Boating and water skiing are popular on the lake during the short summer season. Water recreation and bicycle rentals are available at a number of businesses that line Garden City's main drag, Bear Lake Boulevard. **Bear Lake State Park** hosts three campgrounds on the lakeshore; **Bear Lake Marina** has fifteen sites and harbor and docking facilities, **Rendezvous Beach** has great sand and 138 sites; and **Eastside** has primitive camping in an isolated setting. Rendezvous Beach hosts an old-time **Mountain Man Rendezvous** the second weekend of September. This festival celebrates the gathering held annually on

TOP ANNUAL EVENTS FOR THE FAMILY IN NORTHERN UTAH

Mountain Man Rendezvous, April, Bear Lake State Park, (801) 946–3343

Re-enactment of the driving of the golden spike at Golden Spike, May, National Historic Monument, (801) 471–2209

Festival of the American West, August, Logan, (800) 225–FEST

Raspberry Days, August, Garden City, (800) 448–BEAR

Christmas Parade and lighting of Christmas Village, November, Ogden, (801) 629–8214

---

this spot from 1825 to 1840. Eat, drink, and test your frontier skills with costumed mountain men. Call the park at (801) 946–3343 for dates and a calendar of events. Day use and camping fees are charged. Reservations for state park campsites are advised; call (800) 322–3770 from 8:00 a.m. to 5:00 p.m., Monday through Friday. A dozen other private campgrounds and overnight facilities operate on the lake as well. Camping is allowed only in specified areas on the shores of Bear Lake.

About a dozen businesses in town offer all kinds of rentals and guided adventures. Call the Bear Lake Convention and Visitors Bureau for more information at (800) 448–BEAR.

A local theater group takes up residence in town during the summer months. The **Pickleville Playhouse** offers Western cook-out dinners along with melodrama-style plays, on Thursday, Friday, and Saturday as well as Monday in July. Call (801) 946–2918 for rates and a playlist.

If your family desires a unique-in-the-world fishing opportunity, come to Bear Lake in winter for the **Bonneville cisco run.** Cisco are a tiny fish, similar to smelt, that are found only in Bear Lake. The fish come to shallow water to spawn in late January and early February, and during this time it is possible to cut a hole in the ice and scoop them up with nets. If your family enjoys snowmobiling, there are over 200 miles of groomed trails in the hills surrounding Garden City. Several full-service rental outlets are found here.

The road north from Garden City leads to Idaho. If you continue on this way, a good choice for a summertime family outing is **Minnetonka Cave** near the town of Paris.

SMITHFIELD

The popular **Stage Stop Theatre**, at 141 North Main, offers family-oriented comedies and musicals throughout the year. Ticket prices range from $5.00 to $9.00, depending on the night you attend and the age of your family member. The theater is open Monday through Saturday in summer, with reduced hours in winter. Call (800) 248–2530 for a playlist.

RICHMOND

For a behind-the-scenes view of "real" ranch life in the West, visit this community during the second weekend in May. Holstein cows have been thriving on the green pastures here since 1904, and the town celebrates its prize stock each year with **Black and White Days**. Much of the activity centers around cattle competition; your family, however, will enjoy the fun town parade and food stands. For more information, call (801) 258–2092.

CLARKSTON

For two weeks in August, this quiet farming community greets thousands of visitors to its **Martin Harris Pageant**, a tribute to one of Utah's more colorful Mormon pioneer leaders. Harris spent the last years of his life here and is buried in the town cemetery. The pageant begins at 8:15 P.M. in the outdoor Martin Harris Memorial Theater. Before the show, dinner can be purchased in the nearby Mormon Church for $5.00. There is no admission fee for the pageant, but reserved tickets are required. Tickets are available only by writing to Martin Harris Pageant, P.O. Box 151, Clarkson, UT 84305. For a recorded message on pageant dates and directions, call (801) 563–0059.

In late June Clarkston hosts **Pony Express Days** with a re-enactment of the thrilling horse and rider system that once moved the mail in this part of the country. Ask locally for specific dates or call (801) 752-2161 for information.

COVE

If any of your family are dedicated horsepeople, check out **Hummingbird Hill Trail Rides** in this remote farming community. This outfit offers all sorts of customized rides, including sunrise, campfire and dinner, date, and lunch outings in the surrounding canyons and hills. Rates begin at $12.00 an hour per person for a family of four. This is not an easy place to find, and it's recommended that you call ahead for availability and directions: (801) 258-2025.

Greater Salt Lake

The city of Salt Lake is actually a small urban corner of a much larger area known as the Salt Lake Valley. This outlying valley houses a dozen or so suburbs that have turned into one of the fastest-growing population centers in the country. Cities with names like Sandy and West Jordan boast clean, safe, and rural lifestyles and a citizenry of large, young families. This chapter also describes the canyons immediately surrounding the valley as well as the vast area west of Salt Lake City known as the Great Basin.

The Greater Salt Lake area sports resorts famous for world-class skiing, a treasure trove of Mormon history, a multitude of fine arts entertainment, and, of course, its namesake, the Great Salt Lake. There are two major indoor malls in the heart of downtown Salt Lake City, a hundred boutiques and specialty shops, and many fine restaurants, representing almost every ethnic derivation.

Salt Lake City is the world's chosen site for the 2002 Winter Olympics, confirming the area's claim of "The Greatest Snow on Earth." This honor will boost both the city's name recognition and visitation, and by the next decade the quiet, western town that used to be Salt Lake will most likely be changed forever.

SALT LAKE CITY

"This is the right place," said Mormon Church Leader Brigham Young when he first saw this valley. The date was July 24, 1847, and Young was the leader of a band of road-weary church faithful who had wagon-trained

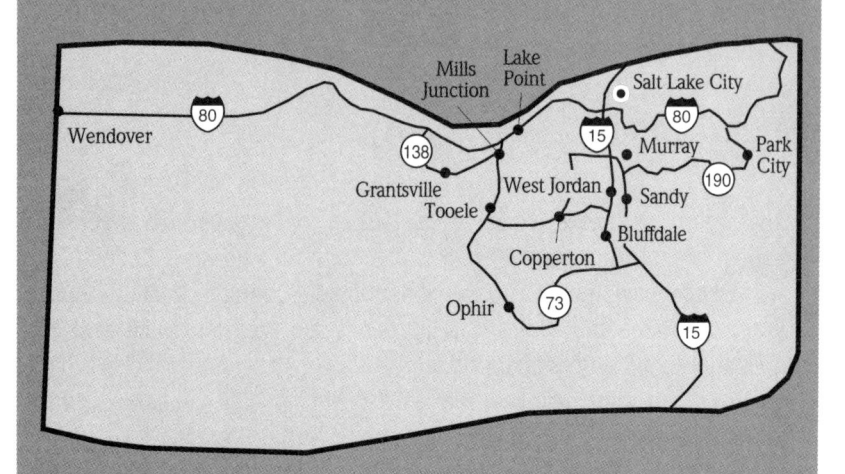

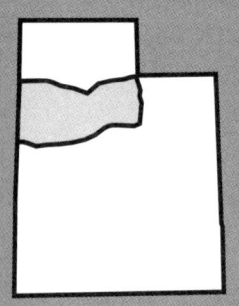

Greater Salt Lake

from Illinois, determined to find a home for themselves. Brigham Young and his followers were wildly successful in establishing an oasis in this desert country, and today Salt Lake remains, perhaps, most famous as headquarters of the Church of Jesus Christ of Latter-Day Saints, better known as the Mormons. Young's legacy provides a well-planned city for those who live here and a fascinating glimpse of history for those who visit.

Most of the central area of downtown Salt Lake City is owned by the Mormon Church, including world-famous **Temple Square** and its surrounding museums, which are visited annually by more than four million people. The ten-acre square is located, literally, in the center of the city, and three surrounding roads bear its name—North, West, and South Temple streets. An original church surveyor's marker can be seen on the southeast corner of Temple Square, designating that site as the exact center of the city. This square block is the most visited space in Utah, revered for its beauty and beloved for its spiritual significance. Not surprisingly, the very first Mormon temple is here, built from granite quarried in local canyons. The first day after the Mormons' arrival in the valley, this square was measured by Brigham Young's walking step and set aside as sacred ground. Work on the temple was begun in 1853, and its completion took almost forty years. Today, only church faithful are allowed inside, but anyone can admire its lovely architecture. Note the golden angel sounding his horn on top of the temple—this is Maroni, honored here for his major role in church history.

There are several other places to visit within the square, and tourists are welcome at all of them. If you would like a guided tour of the Square, walk inside the gates and find the **Seagull Monument,** a stone spire topped by stone seagulls and surrounded by a pond. Tours begin here every few minutes from 8:00 A.M. to 10:00 P.M. in summer and 9:00 A.M. to 9:00 P.M. in cold-weather months. Not only did the Mormons choose to honor the seagull in a monument, but it is also the official state bird. This stems from the bird's early role in church history, when seagulls stopped a nasty invasion of crickets. Just west of Seagull Monument is **Assembly Hall**, built in 1880. A classical concert series is held here on weeknights, year-round, with 7:30 P.M. performances. Tickets are not required and there is no admission fee; however, children under eight are not invited. Call (801) 240–2534 for a concert schedule.

Across the way is the famed **Mormon Tabernacle**, home to the even more-famous **Mormon Tabernacle Choir**. This domed building is known for having perfect acoustics, as well as a 12,000-pipe organ. When your family is inside the Tabernacle, note the pillars that line the aisles. When this building was constructed in 1863, the prized hardwoods of the time were not to be found in this area. What you see is actually the lowly pine, painted to look like oak. When your family visits other Mormon buildings built around this time, look for other replications of materials—such as sandstone painted to look like marble. The Tabernacle seats 6,500 people for Mormon Tabernacle Choir rehearsals each Thursday at 8:00 P.M. and for performances Sunday mornings at 9:30. These Sunday performances are broadcast live around the world on a radio show known as "Music and the Spoken Word" and require the audience to be seated by 9:15 A.M. Half-hour organ recitals, sans choir, are given Monday through Saturday at noon and Sunday at 2:00 P.M. Two **Visitor Centers** are located within Temple Square, offering pamphlets, short lectures, and movies that describe the Mormon Church's teachings and history. The visitor centers are open every day in the summer from 8:00 A.M. to 10:00 P.M. and during the winter months from 9:00 A.M. to 9:00 P.M. Throughout the month of December, Temple Square is transformed into fairyland, when more than 500,000 tiny colored lights are draped over trees and bushes and arranged in patterns in the flower beds. A larger-than-life nativity scene depicts the birth of Christ, and special performances are given each night in the Tabernacle. All tours and events are free to the public. For more information on Temple Square, call (801) 240–4872.

Immediately surrounding Temple Square are several other important Mormon Church buildings that your family will enjoy visiting. Do take time to visit the **Joseph Smith Memorial Building** just east of, and across the street from, Temple Square at the corner of South Temple and Main streets. This grand old structure operated as the Hotel Utah from 1911 to 1987, and in its time was one of the most famous hotels in the West. Recently the building has undergone a $45 million renovation and now serves as an office building for Mormon leaders and a showcase for church history. If you would like to view a fifty-three-minute film dramatizing the story of Joseph Smith, the fourteen-year-old boy who founded the Mormon

Church and became its first prophet, find a small room in the rear of the lobby and receive free tickets for *Legacy,* which is shown on the second floor of this building. *Note:* Tickets are for specific times only. You might consider obtaining your tickets at the beginning of your tour, to assure a showing that fits your schedule. While you are waiting to watch the film, walk through the lobby and around the northeast corner, and you will find the **Family Search Center**. This wonderfully educational place is a "Genealogy 101" for dabblers in family history. The Mormon Church is a world leader in tracing family lineage, and your personal history is most likely contained in the massive memory system here. Find an empty desk and sit at a computer. Within three or four minutes your children should experience the thrill of calling up at least one of your forebears and from there finding the names, birthplaces, and birthdates of six generations of your ancestors. For a nickel a copy, you can take this information home. Top off your visit to the Joseph Smith Building with an elevator ride to the tenth floor, where magnificent views of Salt Lake City are revealed from the east and west windows, and two restaurants serve lunch and dinner. For details on all activities at this facility, call (801) 240–1266.

Don't lag behind. There is plenty more Mormon history to be viewed within a block's walk. A few doors east of the Joseph Smith Memorial Building, at 67 East South Temple, is a favorite visiting place for children. **The Beehive House** was built in 1854 as a home for the second president of the Mormon Church, Brigham Young, and his family. Dozens of pioneer children grew up in this home, and their way of life is charmingly displayed through the furnishing and artifacts that remain. The house has been restored as a museum, and with a guide you can view the bedrooms, books, toys, in-home school, and eating areas that were used by a Mormon family 150 years ago. Original to the house, and part of the museum, is a dry goods store, where old-fashioned horehound candy can be purchased. The Beehive House is open Monday through Saturday from 9:30 A.M. to 6:30 P.M. June through August and until 4:30 P.M. the rest of the year; Sunday hours are 10:00 A.M. to 1:00 P.M. There is no admission fee. Call (801) 240–2671 for more information.

As you make your way around the state of Utah, you might notice that the bee and the beehive are repeated themes in many areas' architecture.

In fact, the beehive is the state symbol, stemming from Brigham Young's admiration for the industrious way bees live and work together. As you leave the Beehive House, notice the carved beehive that sits on top of the roof's cupola. Just next door is a building with a carved lion crouched above the main entrance. This, indeed, is the **Lion House**, originally built to house Brigham Young's extended family. It is not open to visitors, although visitors may dine inside at the Pantry Restaurant.

From outside the Lion House, head a few steps east and view the span of the **Eagle Gate** that decorates the intersection at State and South Temple streets. A 6,000-pound eagle with a wingspan of 20 feet guards what was once the entrance to Brigham Young's property. This is the third incarnation of the original. It has been expanded over the years to accommodate wagon traffic, trolley cars, and, finally, the automobile. The original wooden eagle can be seen at the Pioneer Memorial Museum, which is described later in this chapter (see page 39).

From this intersection, you can head due north for a block's walk to the **LDS Church Office Building** at 50 East North Temple, or you can take a more scenic route by heading a half-block west, and cutting through the gorgeous gardens and fountains that announce the building's formal entrance. This is where official church business takes place, and tourist traffic is not routine. This is also the city's tallest building, and the two observation decks on the twenty-sixth floor offer incredible views of the entire valley. Find the elevator bank in the middle of the downstairs lobby and take the express car to the top floor. If you would like a tour of this building, a free one can be arranged by calling (801) 240–3789.

For the final two stops on this tour of Temple Square and its environs, head west, back through the grounds of Temple Square, and emerge on West Temple. Cross the street to the **Family History Library** at 35 North West Temple. Remember your family history experience on the computers at the Joseph Smith Building? That was only an introduction to genealogy. What goes on here is much more complex. Housed inside this building is the world's largest collection of genealogical records, and people come from all over the world to compile their family histories. If you decide to delve deeper into your family tree, consult the trained staff and volunteers who are on duty here. There is no fee for this service. Tours of the building are available. The library opens every morning except Sunday at 7:30 and closes at 6:00 P.M. on Monday, 10:00 P.M. Tuesday through Friday, and 5:00 P.M. on Saturday.

Directly north of the library is the **Museum of Church History and Art**, at 45 West North Temple. Displayed here are all sorts of interesting artifacts and memorabilia from the pioneer past. One second-floor exhibit honors each of the LDS Church presidents, and another shows a permanent collection of paintings by Mormon artists. Hours are Monday through Friday 9:00 A.M. to 9:00 P.M., weekends 10:00 A.M. to 7:00 P.M., and holidays 10:00 A.M. to 7:00 P.M. For tours or information, call (801) 240–3310.

There is plenty to do and see in downtown Salt Lake City of a less ecclesiastical nature. Two huge indoor malls are located across the street from each other, facing Main Street at its intersection with South Temple. **The ZCMI Center** is named after the original mercantile, Zions Cooperative Mercantile Institution, which sat on this corner in pioneer days. It is now the home to mall anchor ZCMI Department Store, as well as two floors of specialty stores, a food court, and an expansive parking structure. The mall's central courtyard is often the site of traveling exhibitions and seasonal displays, which are of interest to children. The center is open Monday through Friday 10:00 A.M. to 9:00 P.M., Saturday 10:00 A.M. to 6:00 P.M., and closed Sunday. Call (801) 321–8743 for more information. **Crossroads Plaza** houses four floors of specialty stores and restaurants, as well as movie theaters and covered parking. An arcade popular with teenagers is located on the lower level. Hours are Monday through Friday 10:00 A.M. to 9:00 P.M., Saturday 10:00 A.M. to 7:00 P.M., and Sunday noon until 5:00 P.M. Call (801) 531–1799 for more information.

A first-rate planetarium awaits the star buffs in your family at 15 South State Street. **Hansen Planetarium's** spectacular star shows take place in a domed theater filled with comfortable chairs. Individual electronics in each armrest allow the audience to interact with the action above. Two floors of exhibits, including a twenty-four-hour pendulum clock and a moon rock, as well as an innovative gift shop, are also here. Late-night weekend shows feature rock music and corresponding light shows. For schedules and information, call (801) 538–2098.

Family theater is enjoyed year-round at the historic **Promised Valley Playhouse** at 132 South State Street, known as the first playhouse west of the Missouri River. Original plays are performed here as well as adaptations of fairy tales and old-time classics. For a full schedule of events, call (801) 364–5696.

Utah's opera and ballet companies call the **Capitol Theatre** home. This Rococo-style building at 50 West 200 South also hosts touring companies of Broadway plays. For information, call (801) 323–6800.

Salt Lake City is very proud of its new **Salt Palace Convention Center** at 100 South West Temple. This is a busy site for conventions and festivals, and it also houses an excellent **visitor information center**. The staff here can supply maps and brochures as well as give you advice about lodging, dining, transportation, and special events.

Just next door, the **Salt Lake Art Center** at 20 South West Temple has traveling exhibits that emphasize contemporary art in its galleries and a permanent learning space for children on the main level. Kidspace is full of child-sized stations, where hands-on activities amplify the main exhibits. Kidspace is open during art center hours, from 10:00 A.M. to 5:00 P.M. Tuesday through Saturday and 1:00 to 5:00 P.M. Sunday. For a schedule of events, call (801) 328–4201. There is no admission charge, although a $2.00 donation per person is greatly appreciated.

One of the largest rodeos in the world is held annually at the **Delta Center,** 301 West South Temple, in conjunction with **Days of '47,** a statewide celebration of the Mormon pioneers' 1847 arrival in the Salt Lake Valley. The rodeo is one of the highlights of the celebration, with world-champion cowboys and cowgirls competing for $140,000 in prize money. Call (801) 250–3890 for more information on the rodeo and all Days of '47 festivities. The Delta Center is perhaps best known as home to the **Utah Jazz** NBA basketball team. For ticket information and a game schedule, call (801) 355–DUNK. The **Salt Lake Buzz**, the city's AAA baseball team, plays at Franklin Quest Field, 77 West 1300 South, April through mid-September. Call (801) 485–3800 for tickets and information.

A major arts festival is held each June at the **Triad Center**, 350 West South Temple. The **Utah Arts Festival** offers wonderful activities for kids, including interactive science exhibits, face painting, and many arts and crafts projects. Artists from all over the country display their wares, and food booths feature a variety of ethnic meals. Call (801) 322–2428 for dates and information. The amphitheater at Triad is the venue for live performances in warm weather and turns into a skating rink in winter. For information call (801) 532–1350.

At 300 West Rio Grande Street, exhibits that interpret Utah's past are displayed year-round at the **Rio Grande Railroad Depot,** home to the Utah State Historical Society. Rotating collections include artifacts of Utah's Indian culture, a display of early dental and medical offices, and pioneer relics. An excellent bookstore is here as well, specializing in Utah history. Call (801) 533–3500 for current exhibit information and operating hours. Also located in the depot is the **Rio Grande Cafe**, a Mexican restaurant popular with families. Call (801) 364–3302.

When your family is in the mood for a quirky park full of fun things to do, find the **John W. Gallivan Utah Center** at 36 East 200 South. This plaza space in the middle of downtown features a pond that turns into a skating rink in the winter, a huge outdoor chess board, large-sized art projects, and an aviary. Live music at the amphitheater is enjoyed by many brown-baggers at lunchtime and by visitors on many weekend nights as well, weather permitting. Every holiday is a major theme event at this park. For music schedules and skate rental information, call (801) 532–0459.

Washington Square, the historic ten-acre public area between 400 and 500 South on State Street is the site of the **City and County Building,** a sandstone structure built in 1894. For its hundredth birthday the building was given a major restoration, and it is now returned to its ornate Romanesque origins. Free tours are given every Tuesday at noon and every Saturday at 10:00 A.M. Call (801) 533–0858 for information. Fifty years before the City and County Building was constructed, the square served as a campsite for Mormon pioneers who had just arrived in the valley. It became a major social center and was the scene of carnivals, cattle drives, and circuses. The first peace treaty between the Ute and Shoshone Indians was signed here.

Utah's governor resides in the **Kearns Mansion** at 603 East South Temple. This exquisite home was built by a mining magnate in 1900 and was the most elegant Western residence of its time. Guided fifteen-minute tours of the mansion are available May through December on Tuesday and Thursday from 2:00 P.M. to 4:00 P.M. Call (801) 538-1005 for information.

Salt Lake's Capitol Hill area is home to a lovely, old residential area as well as the state's center of government. You will want to start your tour of the hill with a visit to **Council Hall**, located at the northernmost end of State Street. This 130-year-old building saw a lot of Utah's history as the seat of Salt Lake government and the meeting place of the Territorial Legislature. Today it serves another important role as home to Utah's tourism offices. The visitor center here is staffed with professionals armed with directions and maps and brochures to help you on your way. A bookstore in the building sells area-specific maps and guidebooks as well as posters and trinkets. Council Hall is open from 8:00 A.M. to 5:00 P.M. Monday through Friday in winter and Monday through Saturday in summer. By calling (800) 200-1160, you can leave your vacation information requests on a recording and receive mailed information.

Across the street from Council Hall is the impressive **Utah State Capitol,** completed in 1915 and patterned after the nation's capitol in Washington, D.C. The main entrance hall is rimmed with commissioned murals that illustrate the settlement of the Salt Lake Valley. Notice the domed ceiling, which rises 165 feet from the floor. If you look closely, you'll notice that seagulls are painted inside the dome—it is hard to believe, but their seemingly tiny wingspan is 6 feet wide. Statues and busts of Utah's favorite sons and daughters populate the marbled hall. The lower floor of the capitol is lined with Utah history–inspired exhibits. At the eastern end of this level is an exhibit honoring Utah Senator Jake Garn, who orbited the earth aboard the space shuttle *Discovery.* Tours of the Capitol building are available in summer from 6:00 A.M. to 8:00 P.M. and in winter from 8:00 A.M. to 6:00 P.M., seven days a week, every thirty minutes. Meet your tour leader on the lower level by the big map. Call (801) 538-3000 for details.

If you look east of the Capitol grounds, you will notice that the ground drops off steeply just across the street. But if you walk to this hilltop, find a paved path and a set of stairs that lead to the bottom of the hill, and you will find yourself in the heart of **Memory Grove,** a park dedicated to Utah's war veterans. City Creek flows through the middle of this area, surrounded by marble and granite pavilions and a replica of the Liberty Bell. This is a popular picnicking, biking, and jogging area, which extends up the road and into the mountains.

Directly west of the Capitol grounds, and tucked away behind a triangle of traffic, is the **Pioneer Memorial Museum,** a favorite place of children, where all sorts of neat old stuff is found. Four floors of this museum house "the West's most complete collection of authentic nineteenth-century memorabilia," including quilts, furniture, and handmade clothing. Displays interpret early Mormon artifacts, the history of Utah's mining and railroad industries, and Indian artifacts from the period 1847 to 1900. The Carriage House that adjoins the museum displays early transportation vehicles, including the wagon in which Mormon Leader Brigham Young was riding when he first entered the Salt Lake Valley. The museum is open year-round, Monday through Saturday, from 9:00 A.M. to 5:00 P.M. and Sunday, June through August, from 1:00 to 5:00 P.M. Free guided tours, which take about one hour, are available. Call (801) 538–1050 for more information.

You might notice that many of the streets on Capitol Hill take their names from fruit—Quince, Apricot, and so forth. Because of these appellations, this area of town is known as **Marmalade Hill**. The homes here were built by the early tradesmen of the pioneer era, and their many distinctive styles and ornaments make this an interesting area in which to take a walk.

Historic **Trolley Square** is now a shopping center, but its brick walkways and eccentric architecture give clues to its original purpose—a barn for trolley cars. Its huge water tower once held 50,000 gallons of water for fire protection. The square is filled with specialty shops and restaurants and is a fun place to spend an afternoon. It is located at 600 South and 700 East.

Liberty Park is to Salt Lake what Central Park is to New York, albeit a lot smaller. This park is the largest green space in the city center and is filled with all sorts of attractions for children. Open all year are dozens of acres of open area filled with landscaped grounds, tennis courts, and several large playgrounds. In summer an inventive fountain in the middle of the park mimics the mountain canyons to the east of Salt Lake Valley (on a small scale), and shows the path their rivers take to the valley lakes below. Seasonal amusement rides including a merry-go-round and ferris wheel will delight the small children in your family. Older kids will enjoy the walled creative playground, with its two-story slides, sinking ball room, and roped climbing areas. Paddle boats can be rented on the small lake in the park, and a swimming pool is open to everybody.

Many special events are held in the park throughout the year, including the largest **Belly Dance Festival** in the United States each August. In the wooded sixteen acres in the midst of Liberty Park is **Tracy Aviary**. This is America's only public bird park and home to more than one thousand birds from around the world. Even if your children aren't especially interested in birds, they will love the excellent **Free Flying Bird Show** here, where eagles, hawks, and a variety of other birds perform amazing feats for their trainer, in an open-air setting. The show is presented Wednesday through Sunday during the summer and weekends only in the spring and fall. The admission fee to Tracy Aviary of $3.00 for adults and $1.50 for children includes a ticket to the bird show. Call (801) 596–8500 for specific show times. **The Chase Home Museum of Folk Art** is the largest building in the park and is open every day in the summer and weekends in spring and fall. Your family will enjoy the collections of quilts, ranch equipment, woodcarvings, and ethnic arts here. Free concerts featuring local artists are held each Monday in August at 7:00 P.M. There is no admission charge. Call (801) 533–5760 for more information.

The 1,400-acre campus of the **University of Utah** is located at the easternmost boundary of Salt Lake City. Twenty-four thousand students ensure that the campus and its perimeters are a beehive of constant activity. Of special interest to children is the **Utah Museum of Natural History**, with its world-class dinosaur and fossil collections. Your children will love the simulated mine, extensive rock display, biology and anthropology exhibits, and child-centered gift shop here. The museum is located on President's Circle, a one-way loop reached via University Street and 200 South. Call (801) 581–6927 for hours of operation and information on traveling exhibits. Army buffs in your family will enjoy the **Fort Douglas Military Museum** at 32 Potter Street, found by following South Campus Drive to

Fort Douglas. The museum traces the history of this former army fort, founded in 1862 by President Abraham Lincoln. The surrounding grounds contain cannons, former officers' quarters, and a 130-year-old cemetery. Admission is free; the museum is open Tuesday through Saturday from 10:00 A.M. to 4:00 P.M. Call (801) 588-5188 for more information.

A five-minute drive from the museums is **Red Butte Garden and Arboretum,** a wonderful place for children to explore nature. Miles of paved walkways here are surrounded by water, native trees, shrubs, and floral displays. A late-afternoon concert series during the summer draws hundreds of families for picnics on the spacious lawns. Red Butte is open Wednesday through Sunday in winter from 10:00 A.M. to 5:00 P.M. and Tuesday through Sunday in summer from 8:00 A.M. to sunset. Admission is $3.00 for adults and $2.00 for seniors and children. It is located at the far eastern end of Wakara Way, which is reached via Foothill Boulevard at about 400 South.

Close by Red Butte is one of Utah's premier parks, **This Is The Place State Park,** found at 2601 East Sunnyside Avenue. If you remember Brigham Young's words when he first viewed this valley, you will know how the park got its name. This place marks the end of the Mormon Trail, which reaches back 1,300 miles east, all the way to Illinois. It was here that the Mormon pioneers first glimpsed their new home and where Young's prophecy was fulfilled. He had dreamed of this valley, and when he first glimpsed it, he said "This is the right place. Drive on." A large monument honors the pioneers, and a visitor center nearby has three floors of exhibits and information. A well-worth-it fee of about $5.00 is required to pass through the visitor center and on into **Old Deseret Village,** a living historic village that shows everyday life as it was lived in the pioneer era of Utah from 1847 through 1869, when thousands of Mormon faithful made their way to Utah. Farming and domestic chores are performed by costumed docents, and your family can wander freely through the village, spending time where they choose. Activities include adobe brick making, wool carding, and riding in a horse-drawn wagon. You'll see a livery stable, a drug store, a bank, a barbershop, a blacksmith shop, and much, much more. The park visitor center is open daily from 9:00 A.M. to 7:00 P.M. year-round. Old Deseret Village is open daily from 11:00 A.M. to 5:00 P.M. April through the first weekend in October. Call (801) 584-8392 for more information.

Directly across from This Is The Place is the home of 1,200 animals from around the world. **Hogle Zoological Gardens** is Utah's largest zoo and features a giraffe complex, a house for giant apes and another one for smaller monkeys, a circular house for lions and tigers, an elephant building, and hundreds of other exhibits. Discovery Land is a hands-on learning area with arts and crafts, a petting zoo, and a mini-train ride. The zoo is open in summer from 9:00 A.M. to 6:00 P.M. and winter from 9:00 A.M. to 4:30 P.M. Call (801) 582-1631 for admission prices.

Rock climbing is a popular sport in the canyons surrounding Salt Lake. A good place to test your skills is indoors at **Rockreation Sport Climbing Center**, 2074 East 3900 South. Instruction is available for all climbing levels. Call (801) 278-7473.

Across town is a unique set of outdoor floral displays that make up the **International Peace Gardens**. The idea here is to represent, in separate bordered areas, the flowers from different countries around the world. The gardens are located inside Jordan Park, at 1000 South and 900 West, and are open May through November from 8:00 A.M. to dusk. Admission is free.

A hot summer afternoon is well spent at **Raging Waters**, an outdoor collection of eleven pools that features a giant wild wave, a watery roller coaster, and numerous ways to slide into a swimming pool. Smaller children will enjoy a tamer area set aside just for them. Raging Waters is located at 1200 West and 1700 South and is open from Memorial Day weekend until Labor Day. Call (801) 977-8300 for rates and pool hours.

A long tradition of family entertainment continues year-round, Monday through Saturday, at **Hale Center Theater,** 2801 South Main. The comedies and musicals presented here delight audiences of all ages. *A Christmas Carol* plays each December to packed houses, and a special production for children is presented most Saturday mornings. Ticket prices are about $10.00, with lower rates for children. Reservations are suggested. Call (801) 484-9257 for details.

If your children are interested in the goings-on at a working dairy farm, they can join in the daily chores at **Wheeler Historic Farm,** 6351 South 900 East. Turn-of-the-century life has been re-created here, and horses and humans provide the work power. Your children can help milk cows, feed chickens, and gather eggs each afternoon. An original

These feathered friends are just two of the animals you will see at the Hogle Zoo. (Courtesy Utah Travel Council)

Victorian farmhouse is centered on this seventy-five-acre property, complete with a large kitchen garden. Fishing and nature walks are popular, as well as horse-drawn wagon rides. Admission includes a tour. The farm is open year-round from 8:00 A.M. to dusk; however peak season for farming activity is during the warm-weather months. Special events celebrate the holidays. Call (801) 264–2212 for ticket prices and other information.

MURRAY

A popular hang-out for young teens is **Utah Fun Dome**. This indoor cornucopia of mini-golf, bowling, roller skating, baseball, arcade games, and food courts is known as America's entertainment mall. Special events are regularly scheduled, and party rooms may be rented. To reach the Fun Dome, take Interstate 15 to the 53rd South exit, go west to the traffic signal at 700 West, turn north, and 700 West will lead you there. Call (801) 263–2987 for more information.

The **Desert Star Playhouse** at 4861 South State Street offers fun evenings of entertainment for families. Broad comedies and melodramas include much booing and clapping, sing-alongs, and more. You can purchase pizza, soft drinks, and ice cream to eat while you watch the show. Ticket prices are generally under $10.00. Call (801) 266-7600 for a play schedule and show times.

SANDY

The **Sports Park** is a family fun center, featuring outdoor ice skating and arcade video games in winter and go-cart tracks for large and small children, batting cages, and mini-golf during the non-snow months. Prices for each activity differ, but everything costs under $5.00. Find the Sports Park at 8695 South Sandy Parkway, or call (801) 562-4444 for more information.

Salt Lakers are proud of their quick access to the alpine canyons that rim their valley. Within minutes your family can travel from the midst of urban clutter to the wild surround of the mountains. To the east is the Wasatch Range, the westernmost range of the Rocky Mountains, with peaks rising to 12,000 feet. One destination is 15-mile-long **Big Cottonwood Canyon,** famous for **Brighton** and **Solitude,** two ski resorts located near the canyon terminus. Both resorts have plenty of steep terrain for experts, but are beloved by children and cautious parents because of their kinder, gentler beginner hills. Both offer special ski packages and lessons for children, restaurants, lodging, and year-round planned activities. Call (800) 873-5512 to reach the office at Brighton or (801) 943-8309 for recorded information. Solitude's information number is (801) 534-1400. A quarter-mile below Brighton is **Solitude Nordic Center**, a great place for beginners to the sport of cross-country skiing. Rentals anwqd instruction are found here, as well as a half-mile, flat, groomed track with lovely scenery. If your family is ready for more difficult terrain, 15 wild and hilly kilometers of trail branch off the central track. All-day tickets for adults are $9.00. Children under ten ski free. Call (801) 536-5774 for information.

Just to the south of Big Cottonwood is **Little Cottonwood Canyon**, an equally glorious outdoor playground. On your drive up this canyon you will notice the rugged granite walls that rise on either side. This rock was quarried for the exteriors of both the Salt Lake Temple and the state Capitol Building. Little Cottonwood boasts **Alta** and **Snowbird** ski resorts. Utah's first ski resort, Alta is located in Albion Basin, one of the most beautiful mountain surrounds in the world. Snowbird's tram carries 125 skiers on a thrilling ride, straight up 2,900 feet to the top of Hidden Peak. The stunning view here takes in Salt Lake Valley, Heber Valley, and the Uinta and Oquirrh Mountains, and, fortunately for non-skiers, the tram also carries passengers back down the mountain. Both Alta and Snowbird offer plenty of beginner runs and special ski packages for kids as well as lodging and restaurants. Call (801) 742–3333 for Alta information and (801) 742–2222 to reach Snowbird.

During the summer, Big and Little Cottonwood Canyons are much visited by city dwellers seeking relief from the heat. Excellent stream fishing abounds, as well as picnicking, biking, rock climbing, and camping in Forest Service campgrounds. Call (801) 943–1794 for camping information. Hiking in these mountains is a wonderful family activity. The lakes near Brighton are all good destinations and good fishing holes as well. Snowbird's tram runs year-round and eliminates the uphill part of Hidden Peak's hiking trail. However, be aware that the gorgeous downhill route can be challenging for children. The Plaza at Snowbird hosts a summer concert series and during the fall months is the scene for **Oktoberfest.** Albion Basin is world-famous for its wildflower season, in late spring and early fall. Trail maps are available in local stores; call the resorts for more information.

PARK CITY

This resort community is located in Summit County, home to the highest mountains in the state. Park City was settled by prospectors in 1868, and it grew in size and stature as a mining community for more than fifty years. Today the town's **Historic Main Street** retains the spirit of that frontier mining community, with original storefronts that have been carefully restored. Now these buildings hold specialty shops, restaurants, and night spots. A window-shopping walk up or down this busy street is fun any time of day or night. On summer Saturday afternoons, your stroll will be accompanied by outdoor musicians, who play from 1:00 to 4:00 P.M. The **Visitors Center and Museum** chronicles the past of the city, and is found at

528 Main Street in the old territorial jail. Another building to notice on this street is the **Egyptian Theater**, constructed in 1926. Its stage is now used for musicals, dramas, and comedies. Call (801) 649–9371 for performance information. More than a dozen art galleries do a booming business in this area, selling handcrafted jewelry, photographs, watercolors, and sculptures. One of the largest is the **Kimball Art Center** at 638 Park Avenue, just off Main Street. Artists in your family will enjoy the traveling exhibits, the gift shop, and the scheduled arts and crafts classes here. Call (801) 649–8882 for information. The largest arts festival in the state takes place on Main Street during the first weekend in August. More than 200 visual artists display their wares during the **Park City Arts Festival**. Park City has a Cultural Arts Hotline with information on films, concerts, events, and exhibits: Call (801) 647–9747 for updated information.

A less artsy and more brand-name–type shopping experience is waiting nearby at the **Factory Stores at Park City**. The forty-eight stores here service the bargain hunter looking for savings on clothes, kitchen ware, linens, books, and more. A children's playground and two restaurants are part of the outdoor mall. It is open from 10:00 A.M. to 9:00 P.M. Monday through Saturday and 11:00 A.M. to 6:00 P.M. on Sunday. Find these stores just off the Interstate 80 turn-off to Park City, at 6699 North Landmark Drive. Call (801) 645–7078 for more information.

When you're through shopping, a fantastic underground experience awaits your family at the **Park City Silver Mine Adventure**. This is a real-life mine, which over the years has produced more than $400 million in silver. The adventure utilizes real equipment and mine shafts to take visitors, via a windowed elevator, 1,500 feet underground—that is farther underground than the Empire State Building is aboveground! *Note:* If you are uncomfortable in enclosed spaces, think twice before you enter the small elevator cage. Those who do make the journey wear slickers to protect clothing and hardhats. Once underground, you will board a mine train and travel $3/4$ of a mile to the exhibit areas, which interpret the incredible workdays of old-time hard-rock miners and display their workrooms and equipment (which includes horses, who used to live underground for years at a time, moving ore cars from place to place). Once you are back aboveground, the adventure continues with eleven exhibits

> **MARGARET'S TOP FAMILY ADVENTURES IN GREATER SALT LAKE**
>
> 1. Temple Square and environs
> 2. This Is The Place State Park
> 3. Great Salt Lake
> 4. Cross-country skiing at Solitude Nordic Center
> 5. Park City Silver Mine Adventure

including an automated miner who talks about his life and times. A gift shop and cafe are nearby. Find the Silver Mine Adventure by following Deer Valley Drive to Guardsman Pass, and driving up this canyon road for 1½ miles. You'll see three yellow buildings that designate the mine; the rear building is where the adventure is located. The fee is $12.95 for adults and $9.95 for children ages four through twelve. Children under four are not allowed underground. Plan to spend at least two hours at this attraction. Call (801) 655–7444 for more information.

A sure summertime favorite for children is the thrilling **Alpine Slide**, located at the Park City Resort Center. This requires a chair-lift ride halfway up the Payday ski run to the top of the slide and a breathless, speedy trip down 3,000 feet of winding concrete track. The slide is open during the summer from 2:00 to 9:00 P.M. Monday through Friday and 11:00 A.M. to 9:00 P.M. on weekends. A pass for one slide costs $6.00, or a five-ride coupon may be purchased for $25.00. After your slide, play a round at **Silver Putt Mini Golf,** also located at the resort center. The hours are the same as the slide, but prices are $5.00 for a single round, or $14.00 for a foursome. Adjacent to the golf course is **Little Miner's Park,** built especially for the very small children in your group. The array of gentle rides and activities here includes a mini-Ferris wheel, train cars, and a set of gliding airplanes. Miner's Park rides are $2.00 each, or $15.00 for a book that is good for ten rides. Call (801) 647-5333 for more information. Guided horseback rides are also available in the area. Call (801) 645-7256 for information.

In winter, the **Park City Ski Area** becomes the largest ski resort in Utah, as well as the official training site for the U.S. ski team. Its promoters say you can "ski an entire weekend and never cover the same run twice." On a cold day your children will appreciate the enclosed (and heated) gondolas that carry skiers to the top of the mountain. Thirteen other lifts operate at the same time, carrying up to 23,000 skiers an hour over the resort's 2,200 acres. Group and private lessons are available for all ages. The Kinderschule program takes advantage of the 3-mile beginner run and teaches children ages three through six. For general information call (801) 649-8111. For accommodations call (800) 222-7275.

The recreation resorts surrounding Park City will play a major role in the 2002 Winter Olympics, with venues for seven events including slalom, giant slalom, Nordic combined, bobsled, and luge. **Deer Valley**'s architecture and atmosphere is modeled after European resorts, and it is known for its luxurious restaurants and accommodations. More than 33 percent of Deer Valley's sixty-seven runs are groomed daily. Its ski school accepts students four years old and up, with group and private classes each day. Child care is offered for younger children. During the summer months a concert series takes place on the lower grassy hills here, and the Sterling Chair Lift takes hikers and bikers (along with their bikes) up to a network of trails. For general information about Deer Valley, call (801) 649-1000. For lodging reservations, call (800) 424-3337.

Wolf Mountain welcomes skiers as well as snowboarders with its five half pipe runs and night snowboard park. Its 1,400 acres encompass sixty-four designated runs and many miles of off-trail routes. Lessons are available for all ages, and a "skiers in diapers" program offers private lessons for children three and under. A popular summer rock concert series keeps the mountain busy year-round. For information call (801) 649-5400.

The **Utah Winter Sports Park** at Bear Hollow is one of the few western resorts devoted to ski jumping. Novices and experts alike can practice flying on the four downhill ski jumps here, as well as enjoy a summer and winter aerial freestyle jump, a half pipe for snowboarding, and a bobsled/luge course. Lessons are available (beginners start out on snow bumps in the park's play area), and scheduled competitions showcase the pros. A day lodge offers a snack bar and rest rooms. These facilities will be reserved for the 2002 Winter Games, but both before and after the Olympics they can be enjoyed by the public. A two-hour ski jumping session is available in winter only, includes an introductory lesson, and costs $20.00 for adults, $12.00 for ages twelve to seventeen, and $8.00 for children twelve and under. Call (801) 649–5447 for more information.

Park City's golf course doubles in the winter as the **White Pine Touring Center,** an 18-kilometer groomed track for cross-country skiers. Choose between flat or rolling terrain or try both, and ski all day for $8.00 for adults, with no charge for children twelve and under. Call (801) 649–8710 for information.

Snowmobile tours are a popular activity in the hills and meadows surrounding Park City. Sleigh rides can be combined with a Western cook-out dinner for an all-evening outing. In warm weather, hiking, biking, and horseback riding in the aspen and pine surroundings are the featured sports. Enjoyed year-round in these parts is hot air ballooning, for a bird's-eye view of northern Utah. Call the **Park City Chamber/Bureau** for a list of outfitters who offer rentals and guides for these activities at (801) 649–6100.

BLUFFDALE

Valley View Riding Stables, at 17000 South 1300 West, offers horseback riding by the hour or by the day in an open, rural setting. The stables are open year-round, every day, from 8:00 A.M. until dusk. Reservations are required during the winter months. Horses are matched to the rider's ability, and guides generally do not accompany the riders. Rates are $15.00 per hour or $60.00 per day. Call (801) 253–9088 for more information.

COPPERTON

This small town is home to the largest open-pit mine in the world. **Kennecott Utah Copper Bingham Canyon Mine** is said to be one of the few man-made constructions that can be seen from space. *Two* Empire

State Buildings could be stacked on top of each other inside this crater. Five billion tons of rock have been removed since 1906, yielding copper, gold, silver, and molybdenum. The **Visitors Center** has fascinating indoor exhibits and a film that explain's the history of mining and outdoor exhibits that display mining equipment. By looking down into the ½-mile-deep, 2 ½ mile-wide excavation, you will see tiny trucks moving their loads inside the mine. The parts of these trucks are displayed here; the tires alone are about 8 feet high. The visitors center is open from April through October from 8:00 A.M. until 8:00 P.M. The $3.00 per car entrance fee is donated to local charities. Call (801) 322-7300 for more information.

Leave time for a stop at **House of Copper,** a truly unique store that sells exclusively copper items. Your children will be amazed at some of the oddments found here—everything from copper chandeliers to rolling pins. Call (801) 569-2822 for information.

WEST JORDAN

In 1877 Archibald Gardner was asked by Brigham Young to build a mill in the south end of Salt Lake Valley. His business prospered and for many years provided flour for the surrounding community. Today his mill is made over into **Gardner Historic Village,** a countrifed emporium brimming with three floors of old-fashioned furniture, accessories, gifts, and restaurants. The surrounding grounds carry on the country theme, where transplanted historic homes are made over into quaint shops. The village can be found at 1095 West 7800 South. Call (801) 566-8903 for more information.

LAKE POINT

This junction, 17 miles west of Salt Lake City on Interstate 80, offers access to the main recreation center for the south shore of the **Great Salt Lake.** But long before you reach Lake Point, you will notice the lake from your car window, stretching endlessly to the north. This is the world-famous inland sea, the largest lake west of the Mississippi, a 2,000-square-mile body of water with a salt content up to twelve times as high as the ocean's. The Great Salt Lake is the water collection point for the vast geographical area called the Great Basin, which encompasses northwestern Utah and much of northern Nevada. The Great Basin has many inflowing water sources but no exits for that water. This circumstance allows minerals and salts to collect in the relatively shallow water and results in many oddities, including Great Salt Lake, the Bonneville Salt Flats, wetlands, springs, and barren deserts. Today the lake supports several industries. Salt, potash, and magnesium are mined from the lake, via evaporative ponds, and used for a variety of purposes. Perhaps the most interesting lake-dependent business is the brine shrimp industry. Brine shrimp are unique to the ecology of the Great Salt Lake, requiring the lake's high salinity to thrive, and, in fact, are the only creatures to survive life in the salty water. The tiny shrimp lay eggs twice a year—in the warm weather a soft-shelled egg and in the cold season an extremely hard-shelled egg. These smaller-than-a-pinhead winter eggs can wash up on the shore, be left stranded for years, be recaptured by the lake, and still manage to hatch. In winter you will see small planes swooping over the lake looking for the blood-red, winter egg deposits—hundreds of millions of eggs floating together, looking almost like an oil slick. Once sited, boats and nets scoop up the eggs by the ton, package them, and send them off to the Far East, where they are rehydrated, hatched, and used for prawn food. The tiny brine shrimp add about $30 million to Utah's economy each year. They are also responsible for the . . . ahem, unique . . . smell that sometimes emanates from the lakeshore.

Here on the south shore of the lake is **Great Salt Lake State Park,** reached by taking exit 104 from I–80 near Lake Point Junction. From the park's sandy beaches you will view a panorama of salty water, mud flats, and islands. If you time your visit at dusk, you will most likely be rewarded with a spectacular sunset. The park is dominated by a turreted building called **Saltair.** The original Saltair building was an extremely popular meeting place in the late 1800s, when trolley cars used to deposit city dwellers for Sunday picnics and nighttime entertainment. That building was destroyed by fire, and the current building is meant to be a re-creation. Concerts are held here, there are food stands open seasonally (usually April through October), and an orientation video for the lake can be viewed here. Nearby, weather permitting, there are also camel rides, bumper boats, mini-car racing, and gift shops galore. The park is open daily 9:00 A.M. to 6:00 P.M. from Memorial Day through Labor Day, with seasonal hours during the rest of the year. A 300-slip sailboat marina provides year-round activity on this lake that never freezes. Seasonal overnight camping is available here, with open showers, rest rooms, and picnic tables. Admission to the state park is free; camping is about $8.00 per night. For more information on Great Salt Lake State Park and its amenities, call (801) 250–1898. Another popular access to the Great Salt Lake is Antelope Island State Park, described in the "Northern Utah" chapter.

MILLS JUNCTION

To reach this historic area, turn south onto State Road 36 from Interstate 80, 4 miles past Lake Point Junction. You will pass **Adobe Rock,** a landmark honoring the Mormon scouts who first viewed this valley in 1847. A spring nearby was a valuable water source for long-ago travelers. Continue south for 1 mile to find the renovated **Historic Benson Grist Mill,** which operated from 1860 to 1940. It was at one time known as "Brigham Young's Mill" and was a primary source of flour for the early pioneers. It is one of the oldest standing buildings in western Utah. The mill has been renovated for tourists, and much of its original equipment can still be seen. It is open from Memorial Day through Labor Day, Tuesday through Saturday, from 10:00 A.M. to 4:00 P.M. Special events commemorating the history of the area are held throughout the season here. Call (801) 882–7678 for more information.

GRANTSVILLE

Head west from Mills Junction on State Route 138 to reach this small town with an important place in Utah history. **The Donner-Reed Museum,** on the corner of Cooley and Clark streets, tells the tale of the ill-fated Donner-Reed party—a group of emigrants who in 1846 formed one of the first wagon trains to attempt crossing the salt desert that surrounds this area. After weeks of thirst and exhaustion, the group did make it across the desert, only to be caught in the Sierra Nevada Mountains by an early winter storm. They were forced to winter in the mountains, digging holes in the snow for shelter. They subsisted on the leather from their shoes and harnesses, and finally, desperately, by eating the flesh of their dead comrades. When spring came, only forty-four of the original eighty-seven members of the group had survived. During their trek across the desert, they abandoned many of their wagons and supplies, and the museum here has collected many of these artifacts. A log cabin and blacksmith shop are also on the premises. Museum tours can be arranged by calling (801) 884-3348 in advance. There is no admission price.

TOOELE

From Grantsville, head back to State Route 36 via State Route 112 to reach Tooele. This name is pronounced "two-ILL-uh," and while its origin is not clear, it may be named after a Goshute Indian Chief named Tuilla. **The Railroad Museum** here is especially fun for children, with its simulated mine and locomotive displays, including an outdoor steam engine, several cabooses, and a dining car. It is located on the corner of Vine and Broadway streets, in the old Tooele Valley Railroad Depot. The museum is open during the summer months only, from Tuesday through Saturday, 10:00 A.M. to 4:00 P.M. Call (801) 882-2836 for more information.

Pioneer Hall, at 35 East Vine, was built in 1867 as a courthouse, and the cabin next door was one of the first constructed in the Tooele Valley. Both are now operated by the Daughters of the Utah Pioneers as a museum and offer displays of artifacts and pictures. These old buildings are open for visitors on Saturday between Memorial Day and Labor Day from 11:00 A.M. to 3:00 P.M. To arrange a tour, call (801) 882-4742.

An easy drive west of town takes your family to **South Willow Canyon** in the Stansbury Mountain Range, open for car and horse traffic during the non-snow months. South Willow is dotted with campgrounds and the higher elevation here makes this a favorite getaway spot from the summer heat. South Willow Creek makes a pleasant meander through the canyon and is stocked with trout for your fishing pleasure. For more information on camping and fishing, call the Wasatch-Cache National Forest Service office at (801) 943-1794. The canyon borders the **Deseret Wilderness Area,** which is set aside for non-motorized traffic. If your children are older and feeling especially hardy, you might attempt the hike to **Deseret Peak**, the highest in the Stansbury Range. This is a lovely, four mile trek up a well-marked trail, but the grade is relentless and near the end the trail becomes quite steep. Those who reach the summit are rewarded with marvelous views in all directions; on a clear day you will see the islands in the Great Salt Lake to the north, Skull Valley and the Deep Creek Mountains to the west, and all of Tooele Valley to the east.

In early June Tooele hosts a perfect-for-children **Arts Festival**, complete with food and craft booths, face painting, story telling, and general good times. The fourth weekend of each September brings the **Festival of the Old West** to the Tooele County Fairgrounds at 400 West 400 North. The festival has three parts: a Rendezvous, a Pow Wow, and a gem and mineral show. For three days mountain men, Native Americans, and other lovers of history converge on Tooele to show off their skills, perform native dances, and sell their wares. Ceremonies of particular interest to children, such as a tomahawk throwing and children's dances are scheduled throughout the festival, so it's wise to call ahead for specific days and times.

For information about special events in Tooele, call or visit the **Tooele County Chamber of Commerce** at 201 North Main Street (upstairs) or call (800) 378–0690.

OPHIR/MERCUR

Travel south from Tooele on State Route 36 and head east when the road becomes State Route 73. **Ophir** was a raucous mining camp one hundred years ago, when gold was discovered in these hills. It has downsized considerably, and now only about thirty families live in this beautiful canyon. Just a few miles south is **Mercur**, another tiny town with a big mining past. This camp was once the second largest gold producer in Utah. During its heyday at the turn of the century, Mercur's 4,000 residents built an opera house, churches, saloons, livery stables, and a city hall. This town twice burned to the ground and was twice rebuilt. In the mid-1980s open-pit gold mining was begun here, and the current owner has established a visitors center that details the town's history and explains the current operations. The **Barrick Mercur Mine Visitors Center** is open daily Memorial Day through Labor Day from 10:00 A.M. to 7:00 P.M. Call (801)-268-4447 for more information.

WENDOVER

By heading due west on Interstate 80, past Lake Point Junction, you are heading for Wendover and the Nevada border via **Great Salt Lake**

TOP ANNUAL EVENTS FOR THE FAMILY IN GREATER SALT LAKE

Days of '47 Rodeo, July, Delta Center, (801) 250-3890
Festival of the Old West, September, Tooele, (800) 378-0690
Utah Arts Festival, June, Salt Lake City, (801) 322-2428
Oktoberfest, September and October, Snowbird, (801) 742-2222
Christmas lights, December, Temple Square, (801) 240-4872

Desert, known as one of the most barren stretches of land in the country. The road here is dead-on straight; one hundred miles of asphalt with a thousand-mile view circling your window. You are looking at the remains of Lake Bonneville, now shrunk to the parameters of the Great Salt Lake, and the ancient and exceedingly flat lakebed provides an unusual outlook. Optical illusions are common, with mountains seeming to float above the earth and nonexistent pools of water hovering in the distance. If you happen to pass this way during a rainstorm, or in the middle of the sunset hour, the visuals are astounding. In the midst of all this flatness, you will come across one of the more peculiar artistic statements in the world. This desert inspired Swedish artist Karl Momen to weld large metal balls to a gargantuan vertical structure and name it ***The Tree of Life.***

The town of Wendover straddles the Utah-Nevada border, and its Nevada side is a gaming mecca that lures hundreds of thousands of Westerners each year to try their luck at the slot machines and tables. The Utah portion of the town is the gateway to the **Bonneville Salt Flats**, the rock-hard salt beds that provide a perfect venue for car racing. The Salt Flats are the legacy of the above-mentioned Lake Bonneville, a huge ancient lake that once covered most of Utah and parts of several surrounding states. A combination of weather and human meddling have eroded these flats in the last decade, and during the 1990s they may be closed from time to time for reclamation purposes. But most years, in August, this 26,000-acre salt bed attracts the latest in race car technology for seven days of races and events called **Speed Week**. Three additional racing events are scheduled each year during the late-summer months. Call (801) 533–9176 for racing schedules and information.

The old **Wendover Air Base** played a prominent role in World War II, providing the training ground for bomb crews who went on to participate in the first nuclear bombardment in history, which dropped atomic bombs on Hiroshima and Nagasaki. In 1943 this was the world's largest military reserve, with more than 17,000 troops stationed here. It is found by taking exit 2 from Interstate 80 and then taking a left turn at the airport sign onto Main Street. A small museum honoring the military people who worked here is housed in the operations building of Icarus Aviation. A self-guided driving tour will take your family to historic places around the base. The **Enola Gay Monument,** named after the plane from which the first atomic bomb was dropped, is found on Main Street, across from the Peppermill Resort. Call (801) 665–2331 for more information.

Central Utah

Geographically, this part of the state is Utah's melting pot. The alpine scenery from the north is flattening out, but it hasn't yet turned into the red-rock sandstone that dominates the south. This is prime farm and ranch country—and on your travels you'll drive past miles of planted crops and pasture land.

Most of Utah's tourist trade is plied to the north and the south, and this area has a slower, small-town feel. But don't let these rural surroundings fool you. There is much to do and see here, including world-famous rodeos, waterslides, a national park, historic train rides, amusement parks, beaches, and theater under the stars.

The cities below are laid out in a somewhat haphazard pattern, as major roads do not always directly connect the destinations. As the crow flies, the route is circular, beginning and ending in the eastern end of Utah County. Be aware that in the listed order some cities are more than a hundred miles from each other, and backtracking is sometimes required. Consult a road map, and ask locally for directions.

ALPINE

This small residential community is home to **Peppermint Place**, where 600 kinds of candy, along with porcelain dolls, cuckoo clocks, music boxes, and lots of other gifty things are sold. You can take a tour of this cheerful outlet store (and get free candy!) any weekday between 10:00 A.M. and

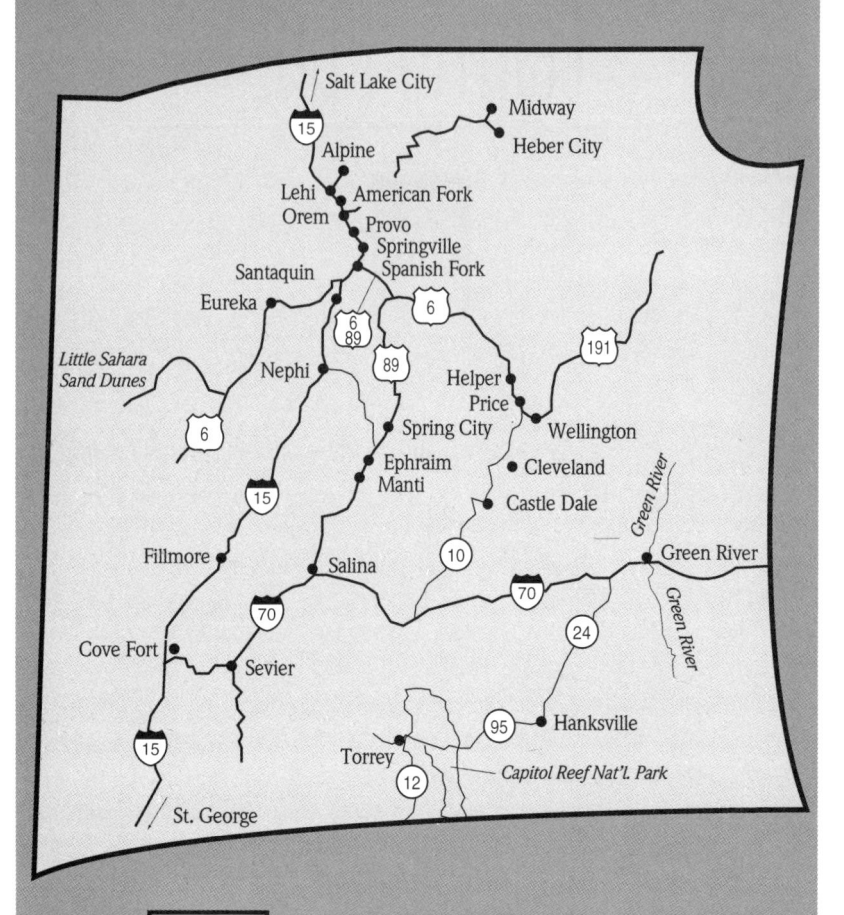

Central Utah

2:00 P.M. From Interstate 15 take exit 287 to Alpine, then find 155 East 200 North. The store is open Monday through Saturday, 10:00 A.M. to 6:00 P.M. Call (801) 756–7400 for tour times.

AMERICAN FORK

For the very small fisherpeople in your family, American Fork has **Paradise Pond** at 1100 West Main Street, a child-sized, stocked body of water, where many kids have caught their first fish. The pond is open weekdays noon until dark and weekends 10:00 A.M. until dark. The cost depends on how many fish you catch. Call (801) 756–6011 for more information.

American Fork Canyon, which begins in the town of American Fork, is one of the most rugged and beautiful canyons in Utah. Three miles up from the canyon entrance, you'll find the trailhead for **Timpanogos Cave National Monument**. A very steep, zigzaggy, $1\frac{1}{2}$-mile hike is required to reach the cave, but the rewards are well worth the effort. On your way you'll have the opportunity to sit at rest areas and enjoy extraordinary views of American Fork Canyon, the Wasatch Range, and Utah Valley. If your children aren't eager hikers, plan plenty of extra time for this climb; you might consider bringing along treats with which to bribe small people "up just one more switchback." Once you reach the cave you'll be greeted by a guide who will take your ticket and escort you through one of the most colorful and multi-formationed caves anywhere. It consists of three primary chambers cluttered with stalactites, stalagmites, draperies, flowstone, and other goodies. Look for the **Great Heart** and the **Chimes Chamber**. Timpanogos Cave is open in the warm season only, from mid-May through Labor Day. The Visitor Center is open, and cave tours are available, from 7:00 A.M. through 5:30 P.M. seven days a week. A $5.00 fee is charged for adults, children pay $4.00, and senior citizens $2.50. Reservations for tours are strongly recommended—mid-day tours, especially, fill up fast. Call (801) 756–5238 or, for advance tickets, write Timpanogos Cave National Monument, R.R. 3, Box 200, American Fork 84003, at least two weeks before your trip. And take a jacket—the cave has a constant temperature of about 45 degrees, the temperature inside a refrigerator. Treats are sold in the lower parking lot June through August, and there are many lovely picnicking sites near the cave trailhead.

Follow the signs from the Timpanogos parking lot to State Road 92 and the famous **Alpine Loop**. This is a spectacular scenic drive that is often compared to a trip in the Canadian Rockies. The views of Timpanogos and Lone Peak Wilderness areas are stunning, and fall color enthusiasts come from all over the world to make this drive in September and October. However, be warned—the road is steep and curvy (and narrow!) and may not appeal to small, seatbelted people who can't see out of the window very well. If you do manage to navigate this road all the way to its junction with Provo Canyon, be sure to follow a connecting road to **Cascade Springs**. This small area just off the highway is a pleasant surprise, a natural wonder of crystal-clear, bubbling springs, cascading merrily over limestone terraces. The Forest Service has built a series of boardwalks over the springs, providing first-rate views of the many plants and fish that thrive here. A series of signs interpret the surround. Admission is free. The Alpine Loop continues its winding way down Provo Canyon and into the city of Provo, which is described a few paragraphs below. The Alpine Loop is closed during mid-winter.

HEBER

Railroad buffs in your family will love the history and authenticity of the **Heber Valley Historic Railroad**. This service still runs old-time trains up and down Provo Canyon and through the Heber Valley, just as it has for almost a hundred years. Once a vital link between Heber and Provo for the transportation of passengers and sheep, the railroad now is fully turned over to sightseers and recreationists. In the last decades railroad enthusiasts have overseen the complete restoration of several vintage coaches and open-air cars, as well as a working steam locomotive originally built in 1904. From May through October you can choose from two round-trip excursions that leave Heber City twice daily. A two-hour trip travels through the farmlands of Heber Valley and along the shores of Deer Creek Reservoir. A longer, three-and-a-half-hour trip continues from the reservoir, follows the Provo River down Provo Canyon, and terminates at Vivian Park. Vivian Park also serves as an on-board location (and is a wonderful place for a picnic!). Snacks may be purchased on board. The train does run in the winter months, but with a reduced schedule. A special "Santa Claus

Express" runs from the end of November through Christmas. Train fare varies for the different routes, and is between $6.00 and $20.00 for adults, $4.00 and $14.00 for children. Departure times vary. The Heber station is located at 450 South 600 West. Call (801) 654–5601 for details.

If your family is feeling particularly adventurous, you might want to check out a glider ride, offered by several local companies, including **Soar Utah.** Family members sit in the back seat, and a pilot guides the engineless plane from the cockpit. "Intro" rides cost between $25.00 and $75.00, and last between ten and fifteen minutes. This service is offered May through October. Soar Utah's number is (801) 654–0654.

Deer Creek Reservoir and State Park, located south of Heber on Highway 189, is a 7-mile-long water recreation area popular with windsurfers, sailors, and boaters. It's also a primary source of water for both Utah and Salt Lake valleys. Facilities at Deer Creek include a launching ramp, docks, campground, rest rooms, and showers. There are camping and day-use fees. Call (801) 654–0171 for information.

MIDWAY

Midway is just down the road from Heber and shares the same green valley. This town calls itself "Little Switzerland," because of both its favorable geographic comparisons with that country, and its large number of residents who share a Swiss heritage. This proud fact translates each Labor Day weekend to **Swiss Days,** one of the state's most popular festivals. Thousands of people flock to Midway for food, entertainment, and homemade craft items. For more information, write Swiss Days, Box 428, Midway 84049.

The **Homestead Resort** at 700 North Homestead Drive is a wonderful destination for families that provides lodging, horseback riding, tennis, bicycle paths, hiking, golf, hayrides, and hot-air ballooning. An indoor heated swimming pool makes for a relaxing soak and swim at the end of the day. The Homestead is a good choice for a winter vacation, with miles of groomed cross-country ski trails just steep enough for children. Horse-drawn sleigh rides and dinner rides are also available. Call (801) 654–1102.

Old-time Utahns will remember the "hot pots," a bowled depression in the Heber Valley with a miraculous bubbling of hot mineral pools. Today the **Mountain Spaa Resort,** at 800 North Mountain Spaa Lane, encompasses some of the old hot pots, with indoor and outdoor pools that are constantly fed with naturally hot (90 degree) mineral water. Cabins may be rented here, and camping is available. An old-fashioned soda fountain dispenses ice cream treats, and a snack bar has sandwiches. Admission to the pools is $2.50 per person. The resort is open during warm weather months only. Call (801) 654-0721 for more information.

Utah's largest and busiest state park, **Wasatch Mountain State Park,** is here, with camping, picnicking, miles of hiking and biking trails, a children's fishing pond, and a twenty-seven-hole golf course. If your family enjoys wildlife watching, this park is a good destination; big game are abundant here, along with waterfowl, shorebirds, and small mammals. In winter cross-country skiing and snowmobiling are popular activities. Each February, snow permitting, brings sled dog races to the park. The races begin and end at the golf course pro shop, and your family will enjoy watching from the deck while drinking hot chocolate. Wasatch Mountain State Park has a visitor center, with directions, maps, travel guides, and local information. It is open 8:00 A.M. to 5:00 P.M. daily. Day-use and camping fees are charged. For more information call (801) 654-1791.

LEHI

One man's love of collecting has resulted in one of the more likable museums in the state. **John Hutchings Museum of Natural History,** at 55 North Center Street, features just about anything that is related to the American West. Your children will love the Native American and pioneer artifacts, as well as the rare rock specimens, fossils, and marine and bird exhibits. A gift shop sells items that relate to the exhibits. John Hutchings died in 1977, and today the museum is run by his son Harold, who continues a sense of family history. It is open Monday through Saturday from 9:30 A.M. to 5:00 P.M. Admission is by donation, at a suggested rate of $2.00 for adults and $1.00 for children. Call (801) 768-7180 for more information.

A few miles from town is a back-to-nature get-away called **Thanksgiving Point Botanical Gardens,** which has twelve acres of "idea gardens" through which you and your family can stroll. This is especially dramatic at Christmastime, when the gardens are decorated with a million tiny lights. Your children will probably best like the Animal Park here, with its barnyard atmosphere and stables full of rabbits, goats, ducks, pigs, baby chicks, and even llamas and a buffalo. A $1.00 per person donation is suggested, which goes for animal food. A garden center, gift shop, and restaurant are also here as is an old-fashioned soda fountain where shakes and sundaes can be enjoyed. To find the Gardens, take Exit 287 from I-15, and go west on the frontage road for about a mile to 2095 North West Frontage Road. Call (801) 768-2300 for more information.

If your family likes to shop, don't miss the funky **Broadbents Family Department Store** at 128 North 100 East, a 110-year-old mercantile with labyrinthine rooms filled with, well, everything. The Broadbent family has managed this store continuously since 1882, and today they sell much of the same type of merchandise that they did back then.

You'll likely notice the huge **Lehi Roller Mills** while you're here. These mills were built in 1905 and at that time boasted the most modern grain processing equipment of their time. The mill continues its original purpose, having been expanded and modernized over the years.

Lehi is famous for its June **Round-up Rodeo,** which has been thrilling folks for almost sixty years. Cowboys and cowgirls from all over the country come to Lehi to test their skills and to take part in the carnivals, parade, and good food that are all a part of the round-up. Call (801) 768-7100 for dates.

FAIRFIELD

Fairfield is a small farming town today, but 150 years ago it was witness to a particularly rowdy era in Utah's history. In 1858 then-president Buchanan sent 5,600 soldiers to Utah to break up a perceived Mormon Rebellion. After negotiations with Mormon leaders, the army agreed to locate close enough to Salt Lake City to keep an eye on the citizenry, but far enough away to not seem oppressive. That location proved to be Fairfield, and the army's home became **Camp Floyd**, now an historic state park. Back then Fairfield boasted more than 300 buildings and was a typical hell-raising, frontier settlement. Today your family can visit the only building left standing, the commissary, as well as the army cemetery where eighty-four soldiers are buried.

While you are standing on Highway 73, the main road through Fairfield, imagine a horse galloping past at high speed, carrying bags marked U.S. MAIL. The horse is the best that money can buy, and its rider, a boy, is wearing a bright red shirt and blue pants and is carrying a small brass horn that he blows to signal his arrival. The boy, of course, is a Pony Express rider, and this route served as **The Pony Express Trail** for nineteen months in 1860 and 1861. The invention of the telegraph ended the need for a horse-and-rider-mail-delivery system.

Visit **Stagecoach Inn State Park** to see where Pony Express riders exchanged mail and stopped to rest. This historic inn was built in 1855 and also served travelers on the Overland Trail. Both Camp Floyd and Stagecoach Inn are open Easter weekend through October 31. Call (801) 768–8932 for more information. If your children are captivated by the lore of the Pony Express, you might want to head out on a 133-mile-long official **Pony Express Trail National Backcountry Byway,** which trailheads at Stagecoach Inn. A number of monuments and buildings along the road tell the history of the Pony Express. If you choose to travel this road, be sure and get a descriptive brochure at Stagecoach Inn and ask for advice—the sand-and-gravel road is not always passable. Call (801) 977–4300 for route information.

OREM

A wonderful, two-day family event takes place each Labor Day weekend in the Orem area. Called the **Timpanogos Storytelling Festival**, it features renowned storytellers from all over the country who come here to dress up, sing, act out, and sometimes just tell the stories that describe their lives and heritage. Typically, the daytime activities include stories interspersed with music and art activities, with food and craft booths nearby. In the evening stories are told at the Scera Shell Theater at 745 South State Street. All-event tickets are about $30.00 for adults, $20.00 for children, with a five-ticket family pass available for $80.00. Children over three only are invited to the festival, and all children are invited only with adult accompaniment. Call (801) 229–7161 for dates, times, and specific locations for the daytime events.

The **Trafalga Fun Center** is a biosphere of recreation activities. Your family could spend a day or more running from one enterprise to the next, including talking basketball hoops, a huge arcade, three eighteen-hole mini golf courses, a miniature race car track, bumper boats, batting cages, and an outdoor water slide . . . whew! Trafalga provides a pavilion, picnic tables, and food service for its patrons. Located at 168 West 1200 North, it is open year-round. Call (801) 225–0195 for more information.

If you have not yet satisfied your indoor recreation urge, move on to **Classic Skating and Waterslides** at 250 South State Street. Bring your own skates or rent them here, and be prepared to roller skate around in a big circle while listening to music. Hours and rates are different every night, but generally the rink is open from about 6:00 to 10:00 P.M. (until midnight on weekends) and there is a family rate of $10.00 for up to eight family members. The outdoor water slide is open from Memorial Day through Labor Day. Call (801) 224–4197 for more information.

PROVO

Provo has one of the prettiest locations of any Utah city. It sits directly below the most rugged mountains in the Wasatch Front, and the view from any city street is straight up and awe-inspiring. All sorts of advance information on what to do and see here can be had by calling the Utah Valley Convention and Visitors Bureau at (800) 222–8824.

Mormon Church–owned **Brigham Young University** is here, the largest private institute of higher education in the world. BYU has an eclectic collection of museums on campus, three of which hold particular appeal for children (and all of which have free admission!). The **Monte L. Bean Life Science Museum** owns huge collections of things-that-were-once-alive, including 200,000 mounted plants, more than a million preserved insects, 6,000 birds, 10,000 fish . . . and much, much more. Children love the exhibits on eggs and shells and enjoy the user-friendly visitor displays and educational programs. Call (801) 378–5051 for information. BYU's **Earth Science Museum** shows off one of the world's largest fossil collections, ranging from Ice Age mammals to ancient sea life and dinosaurs. Call (801) 378–3680. The **Museum of Peoples and Cultures** attempts to trace the anthropology of world cultures. Fascinating exhibits include ancient artifacts and displays from all over the world. Call (801) 378–6112.

BYU campus is also home to two art museums, which have rotating exhibits. The **B. F. Larsen Gallery** (801–378–2881) in the Harris Fine Arts Center highlights contemporary artists, and the lovely, new **Museum of Art** (801–378–2787) features major traveling collections. Most of the BYU museums are open six days a week, and hours vary.

Unique in all the world is Provo's **McCurdy Doll Museum**, an elegant, old carriage house at 246 North 100 East, which has been restored into a home for more than 4,000 dolls, toys, and miniatures. In 1910 Laura McCurdy Clark began a lifetime of collecting dolls, and this museum celebrates her treasures, as well as other collections. You'll see kachinas, provincial Spanish dolls, "rare and glorious boy dolls," ballerina dolls, Japanese dolls, Shirley Temple dolls . . . and many, many more. The museum has a wonderful gift shop full of doll-related paraphernalia, including books, kits, and patterns, as well as a doll hospital for repairs. Hours are Tuesday through Saturday 1:00 to 5:00 P.M. Adults pay $2.00, children under twelve pay $1.00. Call (801) 377–9935 for special events, such as the McCurdy Storytelling Princess, lectures, and craft classes.

Lying serenely at Provo's western boundary, **Utah Lake** is Utah's largest freshwater lake. **Utah Lake State Park** is located on the far western end of Center Street and offers boat ramps, a marina, boat slips, and picnic and food-service facilities. This park is particularly popular with anglers and water skiers; kayakers and canoers enjoy boating adjacent to the Provo River. The state park entrance fee is $3.00 per car. In the winter your family will enjoy ice skating on the park's Olympic-sized rink. The entrance fee is waived, and the cost for skating is $3.00 for adults and $2.00 for children six through eleven. Skate rental is an additional $1.00. Call (801) 375–0731 for more information.

Seven Peaks Water Park boasts the "tallest water slides in the world," and after one look up, your family will most likely believe that claim. Water-park enthusiasts from all over the state come here for high-flying free falls and thrills "beyond compare." There are more than forty-five water attractions from which to choose, including a slide through total blackness, offset by smoke and neon lights, and a tube-hurtling experience that ejects the rider onto a three-story-high, open-air waterfall. For the less venturesome there is a gently flowing "lazy river" and a very nice kiddie pool area. Dominating the park is a huge pool that features regularly timed ocean-like waves. Seven Peaks has an adjacent ten-acre grass and sports complex as well, with food, beverage, and catering facilities. Located at 1330 East 300 North, the water park operates May through September Monday through Saturday, from 11:00 A.M. to 8:00 P.M. The price for an all-day pass is $13.00 for adults, $10.00 for ages four though eleven, and free for toddlers. In the winter Seven Peaks provides a water sport of the frozen variety—a skating rink is open weeknights and Saturdays from about 1:00 to 11:00 P.M. The cost is $4.00 for adults and $3.00 for children ages four through eleven. Skate rental is $1.00. Call (801) 373–8777 for more information.

If your family wants to continue the pursuit of adventure at a high altitude, check out **The Rock Garden,** at 22 South Freedom Boulevard. In this indoor setting you'll learn the basics of rock climbing and the intricacies of the myriad ropes and harnesses and metal clamps that compose climbing equipment. Classes include beginning technique and introduction to lead climbing. Passes can be purchased that allow practice climbing on the simulated canyon walls lining The Rock Garden. Call (801) 375–2388 for more information.

Provo hosts one of the bigger July 4th events in the state, with its **America's Freedom Festival.** This is a month-long hoopla, culminating in a Balloon Festival in the early morning hours, a huge Grande Parade down Center Street, and the biggie—the Stadium of Fire, a fireworks-set-to-rock-music extravaganza at Cougar Stadium, the 65,000-seat amphitheater on the BYU Campus. Call (801) 370–8019 for dates and times.

Provo sets aside one day in the middle of June for small people who love to fish. Bring your children, their rods, reels, and fishing licenses to Footprinters Park at 1150 South 1350 West for the **Huck Finn Day** fishing derby. You will find food, games, and a contest for the most authentic Huck Finn and Becky Thatcher costumes. Call (801) 379–6600 for specific dates and activities.

The city of Provo has the lucky circumstance of sitting near the foot of **Provo Canyon**—a wide, beautiful alpine expanse filled with recreation opportunities. Provo Canyon summits at the top of American Fork Canyon, and the road that connects these areas is called the Alpine Loop (partially described in the section on American Fork). The city of Provo maintains a series of parks with interlinking hiking and biking trails in the canyon. All of these parks have picnic areas, and some have campgrounds and volleyball courts. For reservations and camping information, call (801) 370–8600.

Just a few miles up Provo Canyon is the trailhead for **Squaw Peak Trail**, which offers spectacular views of Utah Valley. A terrific family outing is a short side trip off the main canyon road to **Bridal Veil Falls**, a much-photographed, double cataract waterfall, which takes a plunge from more than 600 feet above the Provo River. The falls takes its name from the intricate, lacy pattern the water makes as it flows over rock boulders.

If you are game for an exciting float trip down the Provo River, strap on a life jacket at Frazier Park, located about half-way up Provo Canyon. **High Country Tours** offers two-hour guided raft trips through the canyon, and all ages are invited. Call (801) 645–7533 for details.

By veering northwest at the junction of Provo Canyon and Highway 92, you'll continue up a side canyon that connects with the Alpine Scenic Loop, described above under the city of American Fork. Several miles up this road is **Sundance Resort,** famous for family skiing in the winter and outdoor theater in the summer. Thespians in your family will enjoy Sundance's **Children's Theater,** a series of open-air summer performances and musicals written and staged just for young people. The series runs through the summer months from Monday through Saturday, with both matinee and evening performances under the stars. Three or four forty-five-minute plays are offered each season, and new plays are presented each year. Call (801) 225–4100 for prices and times. Sundance offers guided horseback rides in the canyon during the warm-weather months. Call (801) 225–4107 for rates. Skiing at Sundance is especially rewarding for young children—long, flattish bowls stretch down the mountain, with opportunities for gentle turnings and incredible mountain views. For skiing information at Sundance, including rates, rentals, and lessons, call (801) 225–4107.

A very pleasant and educational afternoon is waiting for your family on the nature trail hike to **Stewart Falls**. Drive about 2 miles beyond Sundance Resort, and find the pull-out to Aspen Grove on your left. The trailhead is plainly marked and leads you on the 1½-mile walk to the falls. Along the way markers explain the surrounding flora and fauna. You'll return along the same route; allow about two hours for this outing.

SPRINGVILLE

This quiet town, with its wide streets and tall trees, is home to an art museum that documents Utah's art from pioneer days. The **Springville Art Museum,** at 126 East 400 South, was built in 1937. Its nine permanent galleries display about 275 pieces, arranged in chronological order. Most major styles and artists of Utah are represented. Each spring the art museum hosts the **Spring Salon,** a showcase for living Utah artists; it is modeled after the salons in Paris that feature local artists. Older children will love the scale of this museum as well as the historical art that is exhibited here. There is no entrance fee, although the museum welcomes donations. Hours are Tuesday through Saturday, 10:00 A.M. to 5:00 P.M. and Sunday 3:00 to 6:00 P.M. Call (801) 489–2727 for exhibition dates.

The first full week of June Springville hosts **Art City Days,** with a carnival, concerts, baby contest, food and craft booths, a car show, and other fun activities. Call (801) 489–2700 for dates and specific event information.

The **Daughters of the Utah Pioneers Museum** at 126 East 400 South is an historic building that houses mementos from the pioneers including clothing, furniture, handwork, musical instruments, and photographs. The museum is open irregular hours. Call the Springville City offices for specific times at (801) 489–2700.

In a museum you might find fish interpreted as art, but at Springville's **State Fish Hatchery and Game Farm,** 1000 North Main, you will find the real thing. Stroll around the hatchery raceways and view the million-or-so rainbow trout and kokanee salmon that begin life here and are eventually sent to stock Utah's fishable waters. The hatchery is open daily from 8:00 A.M. to 4:30 P.M. There is no admission fee. Call (801) 489–4421 for more information.

Each July Springville offers the opportunity to "travel the world in just one night," with the **Annual Springville World Folkfest,** one of the largest international festivals of folk dance in the world. The week-long event includes nightly performances at the Spring Acres Arts Park at 620 South 1350 East. More than 500 dancers and musicians from around the world dress in native costumes and perform authentic folk melodies and exotic dances reflecting the heritage and culture of their homelands. Tickets are $7.00 for adults, $6.00 for seniors, and $3.00 for children twelve and under. Call (801) 489–2700 for more information.

SPANISH FORK

For a truly unique family outing, head for **Utah Mountain Llamas,** an actual llama "farm" that welcomes visitors who are curious about these South American pack animals. Thirty to forty llamas are generally on the premises, ready to be petted. The animals are also available for pack trips on Utah County trails and for rental as party entertainment. The llamas are deemed "safe and rideable" for youngsters and may be visited at 8628 South Main Street during the spring, summer, and fall. Admission is free; visitors are urged to call ahead at (801) 798–3559 for specific farm conditions.

Each July the **Utah Valley Llama Fest** is held here, a one-day event that celebrates llamas and the South American culture from which they originate. For a dollar entry fee, your family will see llamas sheared and their wool spun and woven into cloth. Continuous South American dances and music are performed and food from that continent is sold. Your children can pet and ride the llamas and get their picture taken while doing so. The llamas also participate in contests of skill, featuring obstacle courses and pack demonstrations. Call (801) 798–3559 for dates and times.

When you need to cool off, head for **Spanish Fork Community Water Park**, found just north of the high school parking lot at 99 North 300 West. The water park has an 18-foot high, 150-foot-long waterslide and a nice picnic area nearby. Call (801) 798–5091 for information.

Canyon View Park is another nice place to spend an afternoon, with a fishing pond for children, nature trails, a picnic area, and playground activities. During the month of December your family can drive through the park and see the **Festival of Lights**, where thousands of colored lights are made into pictures of candy canes, Santas, dinosaurs, skiers, and more. There is a $5.00 per car fee for the festival. The park is found on Power

> **MARGARET'S TOP FAMILY ADVENTURES IN CENTRAL UTAH**
>
> 1. Timpanogos Cave National Monument
> 2. John Hutchings Museum of Natural History
> 3. Seven Peaks Water Park
> 4. Hiking in Capitol Reef National Park
> 5. Goblin Valley State Park

House Road, just past the golf course. For more information, call the Spanish Fork city offices at (801) 798–5000.

HELPER

Fifty years ago trains of heavily-laden coal cars would load in Price and make their way north. Getting up the steep hills of Price Canyon was so difficult that "helper" trains would be attached for a temporary locomotive boost. This tiny town thrived in that era, and its saloons and hotels were famous with the railroading crowd. Helper's old-fashioned Main Street is part of a national historic district and is home to the **Western Mining and Railroad Museum,** at 296 South Main. Your children will love the eccentric collections of early coal and uranium mining paraphernalia, WPA paintings by young, depression-era artists, personal and household artifacts, an old-fashioned dental office (which will make you grateful for modern medicine), a replica of a 1930s store, and two coin-operated model railroads. Outside exhibits include a 1917 railroad caboose and mining equipment that spans a century. Museum hours are Monday through Saturday, 10:00 A.M. to 6:00 P.M., during the warm weather months, and Tuesday through Saturday, noon to 5:00 P.M., in the winter. A donation of $2.00 per person or $5.00 per family is requested. Call (801) 472–3009 for more information.

After touring the museum, the perfect place for a picnic is the **Helper Centennial Parkway.** Find your way behind Main Street to the winding Price River, which is the backdrop for this black-topped pathway, with picnic tables, a sandbox area for children, *bocci* ball courts, and horseshoe pits.

The **Helper Intermountain Theatre** stages live, family-oriented productions during the months of July and August as well as a holiday production in December. While the theater building on Main Street is being renovated, productions are held at the Sally Mauro Elementary School at 20 Second Avenue. Call (800) 842–0789.

It's worth a trip to Helper during the holiday season to witness the **Electric Light Parade**, an extravaganza held on Friday and Saturday nights, the second weekend in December. About 25 floats, lit with thousands of tiny lights, make their way down Main Street while an awestruck crowd watches from the sidewalks. The parade starts at 7:00 P.M. each night, and there is no fee required. Before the event your family is invited to enjoy a chili dinner at Helper's Civic Auditorium at 19 South Main. There is a nominal cost for this meal.

PRICE

Price's thriving industry is coal mining, and you'll see much evidence of the mining trade all over town. In the Municipal Building on Main Street is a famous mural, commissioned by the WPA in 1938, which details the history of the surrounding county. A brochure describing each historically correct scene is available here.

The geology that forced the formation of plentiful coal beds also created the perfect conditions for the preservation of ancient fossils. More complete dinosaur skeletons have been excavated in the area surrounding the town of Price than anywhere else in the United States. The **College of Eastern Utah Prehistoric Museum** at 155 East Main Street displays some of these finds, including full-sized skeletons of dinosaurs and a huge Columbian mammoth in real-life poses. Learn about the discovery of the Utahraptor, the scary, clawed dinosaur featured in the movie *Jurassic Park.* Dinosaur footprints that were fossilized in coal beds are laid out on the floor—your children will most likely want to compare their own size with these ancient bigfoots. The museum also exhibits artifacts of the area's ancient human inhabitants; pictographs and figurines of the Fremont people can be seen here as well. Museum hours are 9:00 A.M. to

6:00 P.M. each day from April through September and 9:00 A.M. to 5:00 P.M in the winter. There is no entrance fee, however a donation of $2.00 per person or $5.00 per family is suggested. Call (801) 637–5060 for more information.

If you are in Price during the first week in May, ask about the activities scheduled for **Pre-History Week**. One day of this week is dedicated especially for children, with games, food, and fun, which might include dinosaur-related crafts and bone-filled "fossil sites" ready to be unearthed. Another annual event your children will enjoy is **Greek Festival Days**, usually the second week in July, when Price celebrates the ethnic heritage of many of its citizens with dancing, authentic food, crafts, and church tours. During the last week of July is the **International Folk Festival**, when Price hosts performers from all over the world, who come to town to perform their native dances. A major rodeo on the pro rider circuit takes place the third week in June at the Carbon County Fairgrounds. The **Black Diamond Stampede** has several events especially for children, including "mutton busting," where local, future rodeo champs test their bareback skills on sheep, trying to stay astride for the longest time. For specific dates and event information for all Price celebrations, call (800) 842–0789.

Horseback rides, by the hour or by the day, can be booked at **Shaman Lodge,** a bed and breakfast facility at 3645 West Gordon Creek Road. Guides will teach your children to saddle, mount, and ride a horse, and, if needed, lead them along the trail. Dutch oven dinners and nighttime cowboy poetry readings are also available by reservation. Call (801) 637–7489 for more information.

When its time to cool off, your children will enjoy the ebb and flow at the **Price City Desert Wave Pool,** found at 240 East 500 North. The giant pool here simulates the ocean's waves at regularly timed intervals. The pool is open year-round, with a bubble covering the pool during winter. Call (801) 637–7946 for hours and admission fees.

A favorite summer escape for Price natives is the **Price Canyon Recreation Area.** Located on a ridge above Price Canyon, if offers cooler temperatures under the shade of ponderosa pines. A self-guided nature trail interprets the surrounding flora, and a campground has picnic tables, barbecues, and rest rooms. Find this BLM-administered area by following Highway 6 north from Price for 12 miles, and turning onto a dirt road at the sign. Call (801) 636–3600 for camping fees and picnic reservations.

A few miles farther north on Highway 6 you'll find the turn-off for **Scofield State Park**, a reservoir that has created a 2,800-acre, high-mountain lake. From Highway 6, turn off onto State Route 96 and proceed for ten more miles to find the lake, which offers excellent boating and year-round fishing. In winter the area is a base for snowmobiling and cross-country skiing. There are three separate facilities that comprise this state park: two full-service campgrounds and a day-use area. For more information call (801) 448–9449.

WELLINGTON

This small town is named after the nearby carbon dioxide gas wells, which for decades have produced gas for the coal, refrigeration, and beverage industries. One of the more interesting backroads in Utah is reached from Wellington. **Nine Mile Canyon** passes through historic ranch country, beautiful cliff walls, and waterfalls; but its most outstanding features are the ancient Indian structures and rock art that line the canyon in profusion. Nine Mile Canyon is actually about 40 miles long—so plan about six hours for this trip, which could include frequent stops, some hiking, and a picnic. From Wellington follow the signs for the canyon, heading north on a paved road that soon turns to gravel. You'll travel about 20 miles until you reach the bridge over Minnie Maude Creek. This bridge marks the unofficial beginning of Nine Mile Canyon. For many years the canyon was the main route between the Uintah Basin (described in "Northeastern Utah") and the railroad in Price. Some of the old ranch houses you see alongside the road were waystations for travelers, where they could stop to rest and water their animals.

Farther on, evidence of the ancient Fremont Indian culture is apparent. The rock structures you see high on the cliff walls are most likely granaries where the Fremont stored their dried crops. The petroglyphs (carvings in the rock) and pictographs (pictures drawn on the rock) you see are their pictorial legacy. More than 1,000 of these sites have been found in the canyon, however if your family is not experienced in finding rock art, it can sometimes be hard to spot. There is a helpful brochure available, which can be obtained by calling (800) 842–0789 or asking at the CEU Museum in Price. A local guide business, **Reflections on the Ancients**, conducts excellent custom tours of Nine Mile Canyon. They are reached at (800) 468-4060. Be aware that this area is extremely remote and there are no services available once you enter the canyon. Be sure to carry water and start out with a full tank of gas. The gravel road may be impassable in bad weather. For road conditions and more information about Nine Mile Canyon, call the BLM office in Price at (801) 636-3600.

CLEVELAND

If you count a junior paleontologist among your family, don't miss the **Cleveland Lloyd Dinosaur Quarry** and its incredible, close-up view of fossil excavation. From Wellington, head south on State Route 6 and take the turn-off onto Highway 10, following the signs to the tiny town of Cleveland and the nearby quarry. More than 12,000 bones, representing seventy different animals have been dug from this site, which has been designated a national natural landmark. The visitor center displays two of these creatures, an allosaurus and a stegosaurus. Other bones from this area are displayed in more than sixty museums worldwide. A short walk from the visitor center leads to a covered area where your children can learn about the excavation process firsthand. Paleontologists continue to remove bones from this site, and their half-unearthed work is on display. Picnic facilities and a self-guided nature trail are nearby. The quarry site is located 30 miles south of Price, and some of the drive is on a gravel road. Before you make the trip, it is recommended that you inquire at the CEU Museum or the local BLM office at 125 South 600 West or call (801) 636-3600, for road conditions, maps, and quarry hours. There is no telephone service at the quarry. Scheduled hours are 10:00 A.M. to 5:00 P.M. daily from Memorial Day through Labor Day, and weekends only 10:00 A.M. to 5:00 P.M. from Easter through Memorial Day.

CASTLE DALE

A really fun family museum is found in this town. The **Emery County Pioneer Museum** authentically re-creates life as it was in pioneer times. The museum has assembled a schoolroom, a typical pioneer home, and a dry goods store exactly as they would have looked in the mid-1800s. Early farming tools are displayed, and a pioneer handcart is outfitted with items the pioneers used for early survival. The museum is found at 93 East 100 North and is open weekdays 10:00 A.M. to 4:00 P.M. and Saturday 1:00 to 4:00 P.M. For more information call (801) 381-5154.

A museum just across the street celebrates the local ecology. The **Museum of the San Rafael,** at 96 North 100 East, features life-size dinosaurs that are mounted on a rotating platform. A group of world-famous Fremont Indian artifacts, the "Sitterud Bundle," is here, along with other cultural and geologic displays. The museum is open weekdays 10:00 A.M. to 4:00 P.M. and Saturday 1:00 to 4:00 P.M. For more information call (801) 381-5252.

Just east of town lies an incredible place called The **San Rafael Swell**; it is one of the more remote regions on the planet. It was formed hundreds of thousands of years ago, when earth shifts created a huge dome of rock. The elements beat on the rock for several eons, until it collapsed into a gigantic pile of rocks, from which canyons and gullies and buttes emerged, creating a "swell" on the landscape. The swell has no services in its huge interior (approximately 60 by 80 miles), but camping, hiking, and sightseeing are extraordinary here.

Inside the swell you'll find a maze of dirt roads that lead to a number of destinations. The **Wedge Overlook** offers an incredible view from atop the San Rafael Gorge. You will look down 600 feet over layers of red canyons into the San Rafael River. The area around the overlook is home to a cactus that doesn't grow anyplace else on earth. The cactus was discovered just a few years ago: it is called *pediocactiwinklerii* (say that twice, fast) after the graduate student who discovered it. (It's also known as the San Rafael cactus.) You'll have to look carefully to find it—it sits flush with the dirt and is about the size of a nickel. This cactus actually recedes into the ground in the winter and has a brief bloom in the spring.

Buckhorn Draw's primary feature is an extraordinary, recently devandalized, rock-art panel. You'll also find towering cliffs, dinosaur footprints, and an unforgettable swinging bridge, which is now used only for foot traffic. One of the few campgrounds in the swell is here, with picnic tables and campsites.

Eagle Canyon Overlook offers a bird's-eye view of **Sid's Mountain Wilderness Study Area,** a formation similar to Zion National Park, which some say is just as beautiful. **Swasey's Cabin** offers a glimpse of the hardships that frontier people endured. Here you'll get a taste of what life was like for the Swasey brothers, who ran cattle in this area more than a hundred years ago. Now, a word of caution: The San Rafael Swell is huge and dry and often empty. Road signs sort of exist, but not enough to depend on. And if it rains, you could be in trouble on some of the less-graded dirt roads. Get directions and weather information before you go. There is a good informational brochure available at any visitor center in the area. For more information call the BLM office in Price at (801) 636–3600. Several local outfitters offer guided trips in the swell, including **San Rafael Trailrides** (801) 637–5510, **Reflections on the Ancients** (800) 468–4060, and **Hondoo Rivers and Trails** (801) 425–3519. The remoteness of the swell can make it seem unfriendly, but it's also what makes this region worth visiting.

GREEN RIVER

Driving down this city's main street, you'll probably notice that many of the businesses here are engaged in the sport of river running. The **Green River** is a world-class rafting river, and it runs right through the middle of this town, which has taken its name. Commercial river trips vary from a few hours to several days, and you can choose an exciting whitewater adventure or a lazy meander under the desert sun. To check out rates, reservations, and individual outfitters, call the **Green River Visitors Center** at (801) 564-3526.

A park on the banks of the river is a favorite starting point for many river trips. **Green River State Park** has beautiful, shaded lawns perfect for a picnic, as well as a full-service campground and boat launching ramp. Day use and camping fees are charged. Call (801) 564-8882 for more information.

Whether or not your family chooses to take a river trip, be sure to stop at the **John Wesley Powell Museum** at 885 East Main, which interprets the history of river running. It is named after the man who first charted the local waters and has a replica of the boat and equipment he used. Also displayed are boats used by early Native Americans, primitive rafts used by early sportspeople, and the modern equipment used today. The geology and geography of the Colorado Plateau (the huge formation which includes much of southeastern Utah) is explained. There is an excellent video presentation here, and a fun gift shop. Hours are 8:00 A.M. to 8:00 P.M. daily, April through October, and 8:00 A.M. to 5:00 P.M. the rest of the year. Admssion is $2.00 for adults, $1.00 for children or $5.00 per family. Call (801) 564-3526 for more information.

Near the museum, on the east bank of the Green River, is a weird-but-wonderful phenomenon, the **Crystal Geyser**. It is a rare, cold-water geyser that erupts at irregular intervals, about three or four times a day. The mineral deposits left by the geyser are interesting to look at any time. To find the geyser, travel east from the museum 1.3 miles, and turn left onto a frontage road. Follow this well-marked road for 10 miles.

Besides river running, Green River is known for growing melons, and each September the entire town makes merry at **Melon Days**. One and all are invited to this celebration, which includes a fair, parade, dances, food, and, of course, plenty of sliced watermelon. For more information call the Green River Visitors Center at (801) 564–3526.

HANKSVILLE

This small desert town is a popular gearing-up spot for the major attractions that surround it. To the south is Lake Powell, to the east is Canyonlands National Park (both described in the Southeastern Utah chapter), and to the east is Capitol Reef National Park (described in the next few pages).

North of town is one of the most unique and fun places for kids anywhere. Travel about 30 miles on Highway 24 and take a left at Temple Mountain Junction to find **Goblin Valley State Park**, a place beloved by children—and with good reason. Their imaginations run wild in this enchanted valley filled with soft limestone hoodoos and elves and goblins. These magical rock sculptures have been carved by the wind and rain over centuries. Look for **Skull in the Sky, Parade of Elephants,** and **Dance of the Dolls** formations. Bike riding is great fun on the long, flat roads in the park, traffic conditions and weather permitting. Campsites are available, as well as a covered picnic area that overlooks the valley. Plan at least a half-day for exploration of the park, with plenty of time for climbing and hiding among the formations. Call (801) 564–3633 for admission fees and seasonal information.

TORREY

For many years this sleepy little town and its adjacent national park remained a Utah secret. In the last decade all that has changed, however, as Torrey thrives with new hotels and restaurants, and visitation at **Capitol Reef National Park** grows by leaps and bounds. This park is a wonderful choice for a family vacation, with a dozen small hikes that offer views up, down, and all around this colorful red-rock sanctuary.

Capitol Reef's defining rock formation is called the **Waterpocket Fold.** In very basic terms, the Waterpocket Fold is a big ridge (100 miles long) that was thrust higher than its surroundings about seventy million years ago. The ridge has one, many-colored steep-cliffed, side, that faces the main road through the park, and another side with a more gradual decline. The "waterpocket" comes from the many erosion-formed depressions in the fold, which are now the natural holding tanks for water after a storm.

Capitol Reef is the most grandiose section of the Waterpocket Fold. The "capitol" comes from huge rocks shaped like government buildings, one rock in particular resembling the capitol building in Washington, D.C. The "reef" designation reportedly comes from the early Anglo explorers of this area. They had seafaring backgrounds, and the reef provided an impenetrable barrier to travel, just as a coral reef in the ocean would bar ships from a direct route.

The most-visited sections of the park extend from the visitor center. Directions to all Capitol Reef hikes and drives can be found here, as well as books, maps, exhibits, and a short film. Bathrooms, drinking water, and a soft drink machine are located just outside. The nearby park campground is beautiful, located along the Fremont River with a surround of spectacular red-rock views. In warm-weather months the first-come, first-served sites are usually gone by midmorning, so it is wise to plan ahead for alternative lodging. For more information on staying in or near the park, write Capitol Reef National Park, Torrey 84775, or call the visitor center at (801) 425–3791.

A favorite haunt in Capitol Reef is the area called **Fruita.** The Fremont River runs through here, creating an oasis in the red-rock desert. A hundred years ago settlers established a township, planting hundreds of fruit trees, and the original orchards are still maintained today. In the fall, visitors are invited to pick fruit for their own use, for a small fee. A brochure in the visitor center will tell you more about the history of this place, but your family can still see a few of the old buildings that remain. One roadside exhibit features an old blacksmith shop, where you can press a button and the blacksmith will tell you his story. The same device is used at the tiny, one-room, log schoolhouse, where Mrs. Torgerson tells us her true-life teaching experiences. The school was built in the 1890s and used until the 1940s. While you're here, think how the world has changed—just fifty years ago children sat in this school and learned to read! You might recognize the beautifully restored hay barn in Fruita, as its photograph graces some of the park publications. Fruita has a large grass area that is perfect for a picnic, a game of frisbee, or an afternoon nap. You will probably notice the abundance of deer in the area, many of which are extremely tame. One deer in particular is fond of getting his picture taken while eating an apple from your hand.

When your family is ready for a hike, grab a **Hickman Trail** pamphlet at the visitor center, so you will be able to interpret each of the eighteen markers along the way. This relatively easy 2-mile-round-trip hike is probably the most popular in the park, and deservedly so. It features 125-foot Hickman Bridge, a spectacular stone arch. Try to be the first one to spot Hickman, as it is camoflouged quite cleverly on its approach. On the way you will pass the foundation of an ancient pit house and granary, probably built by the Fremont Indians. There are all sorts of rock hiding places along the trail, including small rock fins and cliffside depressions the perfect size for a human. Once you reach the bridge, continue on the path. You will loop back around to the original path after a while, but first you'll be treated to good views of Fruita.

Another great hike is called **Grand Wash**—an ancient riverbed that makes for a nice, no-uphill stroll through a magnificent rock canyon. Caution: If it looks like rain, you will want to make other plans. This is not a good place to be during a flash flood. You can start in two places—a

> ## TOP ANNUAL EVENTS
> ## FOR THE FAMILY
> ## IN CENTRAL UTAH
>
> Scandinavian Festival/Heritage Days, Memorial Day weekend, Ephraim and Spring City, (801) 281-4346
> Black Diamond Stampede Rodeo, June, Price, (800) 842-0789
> Timpanogos Storytelling Festival, Labor Day weekend, Orem, (801) 229-7161
> Swiss Days, Labor Day weekend, Midway, (800) 228-8824
> Electric Light Parade, December, Helper, (800) 842-0789

marked pull-off a few miles south of the visitor center, or a marked side road on the Scenic Drive. A one-way trip through Grand Wash is 2.4 miles. Whichever way you begin, you might want to arrange for a car to pick you up at the other end. You'll squeeze through narrow cliff passages, see arches (look up!), find smooth river stones of every possible color, and feel the power of the canyon walls surrounding you.

Just before dusk, try heading to **Sunset Point Trail,** which is, yes, an excellent place to be during a sunset. You might want to take refreshments and make a dinner party out of your visit. Take the turn-off to Panorama Point, park, and take the short walk to Gooseneck Point. Stop and gaze down in wonder at the path Sulphur Creek has wrought, and then continue for a half-mile to Sunset Point. Looking to the east, with the sun at your back, you'll get a good view of the Waterpocket Fold and the pink and orange world beyond.

A wonderful road trip known as the **Scenic Drive** begins at the visitor center, passes through the picnic area and national park campground, and then heads out into desert country. There is a free pamphlet available at the visitor center that is very helpful in interpreting your surroundings.

This is a narrow, twisty road at times, with plenty of pull-outs and short hikes. Eight-or-so miles into the scenic drive, you'll see the sign for **Capitol Gorge,** an especially fun destination for children. Weather permitting, this turn-off onto a graded dirt road is easily managed in a passenger car. There are picnic tables and displays at the trailhead inside Capitol Gorge—this was the main road from Hanksville to Torrey for many years, and some of the trials and tribulations of maintaining the road are documented. There is an easy, 1-mile hike deeper into the narrowness of Capitol Gorge—look for the Pioneer Register, where pioneers signed their names on the rocks, and the natural Water Tanks, which hold good supplies of rain water.

If your family is happy taking a half-day drive on a bumpy dirt road, consider touring **Cathedral Valley**. This area is extremely beautiful, with several unmatched viewpoints—especially memorable are the **Temple of the Sun and Moon** monoliths. Cathedral Valley is named for its many-spired formations that resemble church architecture and also inspire spiritual thoughts. Ask for directions and road conditions at the visitor center. This road requires a high-clearance vehicle, some driving skill, and is not for everybody.

SALINA

You'll find several good reasons to visit this small ranching town. The first is **Mom's Cafe**, on the corner of State and Main, an institution of sorts, where friendly service and old-fashioned, home-cooking reign. Even if you're not hungry, stop in for a scone, one of mom's specialties. When you are feeling well-fed, walk a half-block to **Burn's Saddlery,** at 79 West Main, a "real" cowboy store stocked with all sorts of interesting stuff. The selection of children's cowboy boots is first-rate, and the clerks here know how boots should fit. Some of the ranching equipment for sale is downright confusing to a city slicker—have your children guess the uses of some of the more exotic looking paraphernalia.

SEVIER

Just up the road from this small town is **Fremont Indian State Park**. The park's creation is rather serendipitous—state road crews were clearing a path for Interstate 70 through this area, called Clear Creek Canyon, when they uncovered remnants of an ancient Indian tribe. This park now protects that archaeological find and honors the Fremont tribe, which lived and worked here as early as 3500 B.C. You'll see the Fremonts' pit houses and stone granaries as well as their cliff dwellings built high up on the canyon walls for protection. The park has a museum and exhibit room and twelve interpretive trails that show off Fremont rock-art panels. The park is open daily, except major holidays, from 9:00 A.M. to 6:00 P.M. in the summer and 9:00 A.M. to 5:00 P.M. in winter. A campground and picnic area are nearby. There is an admission fee of $5.00 per vehicle. Call (801) 527–4631 for more information.

COVE FORT

This place is actually an historic site to which a small town has attached itself. **Cove Fort** is one of the better re-creations of pioneer life anywhere. It is located near the junction of Interstates 15 and 70 and is easily found by following the directional signage. Cove Fort's original purpose was as a way station for travelers between the cities of Fillmore and Beaver. The "cove" part of the fort is easy to understand, as there are a steady water supply and a natural rock surround here that lend themselves to a cove designation. The "fort" part of the equation has to do with "Indian troubles" that cropped up around 1867 nearby. Mormon Leader Brigham Young asked that a sturdy rock fort be built, capable of sustaining life within and fending off attacks from without. The fort was built according to his specifications, from rock quarried nearby. It never had to prove its mettle, however, as peace was made with the local Indians, and there was no need for armed shelter. When you pass through the gates of the fort, you'll most likely be greeted by a Mormon guide, who will stay with you during your visit. You'll see a real frontier kitchen, replete with all sorts of utensils. You'll see bedrooms and parlors and eating rooms, all re-created to look just as they did a century ago. Once you leave the fort itself, there are surrounding grounds to explore. Don't miss the blacksmith shop, where a modern-day guide will work the bellows if you ask. The enormous barn has been built to absolute specifications, matching the original that once stood on this spot. This is a nice spot for a picnic, with plank tables set out under big, shady trees. Cove Fort is open every day from 8:00 A.M. to dusk and there is no admission fee. For more information call (801) 438–5547.

FILLMORE

If you look at a map of Utah, you'll notice that Fillmore is almost smack in the center of the state, which might account for Mormon Leader Brigham Young's declaring this town the state capital in 1851. He commissioned an elaborate capitol building, and work commenced. After two years, only the south wing of the building was completed, however, and shortly after the seat of government was transferred to Salt Lake City.

The existing structure, now called **Territorial Statehouse State Park,** served as the site for only one full session of the territorial legislature. It fell into disuse and in 1930 was restored and reopened as a museum. In 1957 it became Utah's first state park. It now houses a collection of pioneer artifacts. Be sure to go to the lower level and find a favorite exhibit of children, an example of an early jailhouse. Outside the building is a picnic area and award-winning rose garden. The statehouse is open seven days a week, from 9:00 A.M. to 6:00 P.M. in the summer and 9:00 A.M. to 5:00 P.M. in winter. There is an entrance fee of $2.00 per person, with children five and under admitted free. For more information, call (801) 743-5316.

MANTI

This tiny town greets 30,000 visitors during the run of its annual, midsummer **Mormon Miracle Pageant,** played out against the dramatic backdrop of Manti's Mormon Temple. This two-week extravaganza requires the volunteer services of just about everybody in town. Hundreds of people are cast in the pageant, which depicts the story of the *Book of Mormon*, and the history of the American continent. Scores more of the townfolk are involved in feeding the influx of visitors; arrive early for the barbecued turkey dinner served at the Manti Tabernacle at 100 South and Main Street, and also at the Manti Stake Center at 300 South and Main Street. The pageant begins at nightfall, about 9:30 P.M. Bring a blanket, as the chairs fill up quickly, and most pageant-watchers sit on the grass. There is no charge for the pageant and a fee of $6.00 for adults and $3.00 for children, 11 and under. Call (801) 835-3000 for specific dates and more information.

EPHRAIM AND SPRING CITY

These towns have separate annual festivals, but as the festivals are always held on the same day, and as the towns are only 10 miles apart, a visit to both makes a nice day trip. Ephraim's **Scandinavian Festival** honors the area's heritage with a Little Denmark supper, booths, crafts, an ugly troll contest, a rodeo, and more. Spring City is a historic Mormon town, with a century of architecture still intact. For its **Heritage Days**, many of the townsfolk open their doors to visitors, allowing a glimpse inside these beautiful old homes. Both of these festivals fall on the Saturday before Memorial Day. Call (801) 281–4346 for more information on both.

NEPHI

Hold on to your hats! One of Utah's largest rodeos is held here, usually during the second weekend of July. The **Ute Stampede's** festivities include a parade with horses, band, and floats, as well as a carnival, foot races, a street dance, and golf tournament. The rodeo features top cowboys and cowgirls from all over the West showing their bareback, roping, bull riding, and barrel racing skills. Its three-night run includes a Thursday Family Night, with a special child's entrance fee of $2.00. Regular tickets are about $10.00. Call (801) 623–4407 for details.

LITTLE SAHARA SAND DUNES

If you continue to travel south from Eureka on Highway 6 for 20 miles, you'll come across the turn-off to a geologic oddity known as **Little Sahara**. This 60,000-acre dune is popular with families who enjoy driving ATVs and dune buggies over the rolling sand. Some areas are fenced off for "sand play," and no vehicles or horses are allowed in these. The dune is a moving force, traveling an incredible 18 inches a year; it is estimated that Little Sahara started out 150 miles from its present location. Sand drags and racing events are held regularly. Four campgrounds surround the dune, as do several picnic areas. A day-use fee of $5.00 per vehicle is charged. Call the BLM for more information at (801) 743–6811.

EUREKA

One hundred and thirty years ago this was a boom town, and a motherlode of gold, silver, lead, and other metals was mined from the nearby mountains. Today Eureka is a living history museum of sorts, a town still standing, but barely inhabited. This area is now called the **Tintic National Historic Mining Area.** Wandering the streets of Eureka and imagining what once was is an interesting way to spend an afternoon. The cemetery near town will appeal to children who are old enough to interpret the stories on the gravestones. The nearby town of Tintic has a nice, little museum that chronicles the area's history. Children especially enjoy a model of the inside of a silver mine. To visit the **Tintic Mining Museum,** you need to make advance arrangements by calling (801) 433–6842, as the museum does not have regular hours of operation.

SANTAQUIN

The charming **Chieftain Museum** here is divided into themes—displaying memorabilia from each and every war veteran in town, a hand cart used by the pioneers, old farm machinery, and more. You'll find this historic building, which was originally built as a schoolhouse, at 100 South 100 West. The museum is open on Friday and Saturday from April through August. There is no admission fee, however donations are encouraged. For more information call the Santaquin City offices at (801) 754–3211.

PAYSON

Payson Canyon is a gateway to the **Nebo Loop Scenic Byway**, which travels through the Uinta National Forest between the cities of Nephi and Payson, up and around the highest mountain in the Wasatch Range—Mount Nebo's 11,877 feet. This 38-mile road is famous for its spectacular views of Utah Valley and the Wasatch Mountains and is particularly popular in September and October with lovers of fall colors. If you travel this road, be sure to pull off when you see the sign for **Devil's Kitchen**. This red-rock formation is most unusual in its alpine surround. The Nebo Loop is very popular with families who enjoy fishing, canoing, and hiking. There are several campgrounds along the road, and many picnic areas.

Payson celebrates the local bounty with **Golden Onion Days** each Labor Day weekend. Carnival rides and booths are open all weekend, and horse races are scheduled for specific days. Call (800) 222–UTAH for more information. The city honors its many Scottish residents with a **Scottish Festival** each July. A parade features Scottish bands, and Highland games and dancing competitions in the city park, at 255 South Main Street. Call (801) 465–2634 for specific dates.

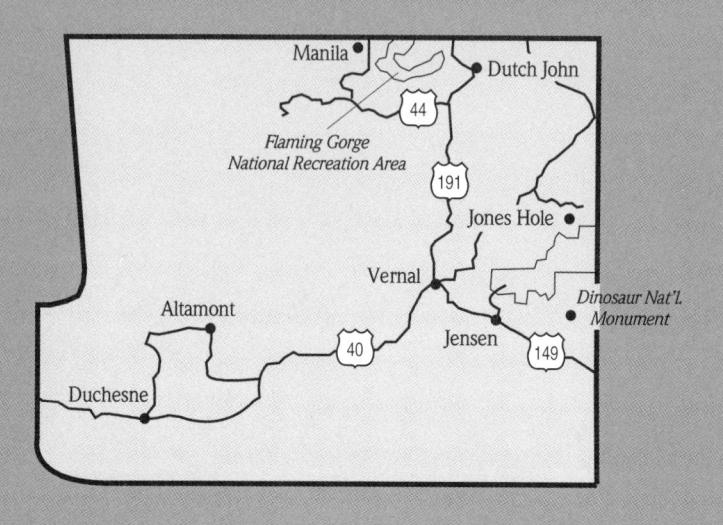

Northeastern Utah

Northeastern Utah

Northeastern Utah is known as dinosaur land. While significant fossil quarries have been found in other parts of Utah (most notably in Emery County), the geographical area known as the Uintah Basin is famous worldwide for the plentitude and pristine condition of its dinosaur fossils. For the dinosaur aficionado, there are quarries and parks and museums devoted to dinosaurs—and even bike and hike trails, rodeos, and dinner menus that pick up on the "terrible lizard" theme. If you want to, you can spend two or three days totally immersing yourself in dinosaur artifacts. If your interests spread to ancient stuff in general, some of the oldest geologic eras on earth are exposed here—you can get your picture taken next to a billion-year-old rock.

The area also boasts Flaming Gorge, a flamboyantly colored rock formation that skirts the trout-laden Green River. When you're near the Green River, remember that the sport of river running was first practiced in this part of Utah and is still going strong today. The Ashley National Forest sprawls across the Uinta Mountains here—home of wild, scenic beauty and excellent stream fishing. If you saw the movie *Butch Cassidy and the Sundance Kid,* you'll want to check out the real-life haunts of Butch and his gang near Vernal, where they headquartered for a time.

DUCHESNE

Much of eastern Utah enjoys the bounty of a petroleum-rich landscape, and as you travel Highway 40 through Duchesne and the other small towns in this part of the state, you will see evidence of the oil industry.

You will also cross two of Utah's major reservoirs and water recreation havens: Strawberry and Starvation dams. **Strawberry Reservoir** is the largest in Utah, with a water surface of 27,000 acres. It is a popular trophy fishing spot, with a lodge, marina (with boat and equipment rentals), and numerous campgrounds on its shores. The Strawberry Visitor Center is a wonderful rest stop, with two short nature trails that are perfect for stretching your legs. One is land-based—look for hawks overhead. The other has a water view leading to a protected part of the reservoir. During spawning seasons (spring and fall), fish are trapped here for a short time while their eggs are harvested, and the fish activity is fast and furious. Call (801) 548–2321 for more information. Just outside of town, **Starvation Reservoir** hosts a state park on its beaches that provides a campground, rest rooms, showers, fish cleaning facilities, and sewage dumps. Call (801) 738–2326.

FORT DUCHESNE

Fort Duchesne still looks like the army post it was in the 1880s, but its modern-day function is serving as headquarters for the 2,500-acre **Uintah-Ouray Indian Reservation**. The Uintah-Ourays host a **Bear Dance** every spring, and if you're lucky enough to be in the area during this three-day festival, do go out of your way to participate. The tribe also hosts a **Pow Wow and All-Indian Rodeo** over the Fourth of July weekend. Call (801) 722–5141 for information on all events at Fort Duchesne.

VERNAL

Vernal is heaven for the dinosaur enthusiast. Just by driving down Main Street, you'll see scores of dinosaurs adorning the town's establishments. Dino motels, restaurants, and gift shops abound (even the taxi service in town is called T-Rex Taxi). If you call the Dinosaurland information office at (800) 477–5558 before your visit, you will be mailed an official "dinosaur hunting license" and a brochure describing the area.

A good first stop for orientation is the **Field House of Natural History,** a Utah state park that also houses a visitor information center. It is located at 235 Main Street in the center of town. Call (801) 789–3799 for information. Natural history displays describe the people who first settled this area; Fremont Indian artifacts and Ute Indian ceremonial clothes

NORTHEASTERN UTAH 89

Get up close and personal with a lifesize triceratops replica at Vernal's Dinosaur Gardens.
(Courtesy Utah Travel Council)

can be seen. A mural describes the geologic formations in the area, which reveal three-billion-year-old rocks. Rocks and fossils are on display; don't miss the fluorescent mineral room. In the visitor center you'll find brochures, videos, maps, and helpful people to explain the area and its attractions. Museum hours are 8:00 A.M. to 9:00 P.M. in summer and 8:00 A.M. to 5:00 P.M. the rest of the year. There is an entrance fee of $2.00 per person or $5.00 per family.

Adjacent to the Field House is **Dinosaur Gardens,** which is (you guessed it) a dinosaur-filled garden. Fifteen life-size sculpted dinosaurs, tinted in authentic hues, roam a two-acre park. Your children will see the terrible tyrannosaurus rex, a pterodactyl, and a Utah raptor, an ancient bird first discovered in this state. The plantings are carefully chosen to imitate food that would have tempted real dinosaurs; a small lake and waterfall echo the more temperate climate that reigned here 200,000 years ago. At night the dinosaurs are lighted, and informational talks are given each evening during the summer. During the month of December thousands of tiny Christmas lights surround the dinosaurs to celebrate the holiday season. Entrance to Dinosaur Gardens is included in the Field House admission.

When you're ready to take a break from dinosaur hunting, there are three other museums in town. Next door to the Field House of Natural History is the **Uintah County Library,** home of the **Ladies of the White House Doll Collection**. This includes a doll representing each of the first ladies of the White House, each doll draped in an authentic reproduction of the gown the president's wife wore at her Inaugural Ball. The collection can be seen six days a week, from 10:00 A.M. to 6:00 P.M. Call (801) 789–0091. Just down the street, at 200 South and 500 West, is the **Daughters of Utah Pioneers Museum**. It contains artifacts and pictures describing the history of the area, from the time Vernal was settled in the 1800s. This museum is open only on summer afternoons. Vernal's biggest and newest museum is the **Western Heritage Museum and Convention Center**. The theme here is the Old West, and there are memorabilia explaining Uintah County's outlaw past, as well as an art gallery and gift shop. Call (801) 789–7399 for hours and more information.

The rock collectors in your family are in for a treat when they visit **Remains to Be Seen** on Main Street (801–789–0100), a sort of rock-shop-elevated-to-art-gallery. Browsing is good here, as fossils and rocks take on exhibit status. Just a few steps away, on the other side of the street, is **Dinah Bowl**, open evenings for families who love to bowl. Call (801) 789–3302 for hours and rates. There are two water slides in town, with the tantalizing names of **Hydrosauras Slide** (801–789–1010) and **Aquanoodle Slide** (801–789–5281). Hours vary according to the season, so call ahead for availability and directions. Older children in your family will enjoy the amenities at **Spring Creek Park**, where teens gather to enjoy each other's company while playing mini golf and video games. Batting cages and a snack bar complete the scene at 1781 West 1000 South. Call (801) 781–0088 for rates and hours.

If you pass this way in midsummer, chances are your visit will coincide with a festival or rodeo celebration. Early June brings **Rough Rider Days** and its rodeo to Roosevelt. The second weekend in July is the **Dinosaur Round-Up Rodeo** and **Dinosaur Days** in Vernal; the rodeo runs for four nights and is billed as one of the biggest and best in the West. Dinosaur Days takes place at the Field House and offers food and craft booths and special activities. Vernal also hosts the **Outlaw Trail Festival** in June and July, with an outdoor play that enlivens local history. For more information all of these events call (800) 477–5558.

Vernal has a dozen motels (less than half have pools). Book ahead during tourist season, because the rooms fill up on weekends. If you're looking for a destination resort, try Red Canyon Lodge or U-Bar Ranch, both about an hour's drive from Vernal, but in different directions. **Red Canyon Lodge** is northwest from Vernal, on Highway 44, perched on the south rim of Red Canyon in the Ashley National Forest. There is a spectacular 1,500-foot overlook here of Flaming Gorge and the Green River that runs through it. The lodge is open most of the year—all of the warm months and on winter weekends for snowmobilers. Dinner here is a treat, to be enjoyed out on the deck or in the wall-to-wall windowed dining room. Look for blue herons and other fabulous birds, chipmunks, and deer. Horseback rides can be arranged, and the lodge keeps a stocked fishing pond for children. Call (801) 889–3759 for reservations. **U-Bar Ranch** sits on the edge of the officially-designated High Uinta Wilderness Area. Here you'll stay in a rustic cabin, share a bathroom with another family, eat

> **MARGARET'S TOP FAMILY ADVENTURES IN NORTHEASTERN UTAH**
>
> 1. Field House of Natural History State Park and Dinosaur Gardens
> 2. Flaming Gorge Dam Visitor Center
> 3. Dinosaur National Monument
> 4. The cabin of cowgirl Josie Bassett Morris
> 5. John Jarvie Historic Ranch

family-style, and truly "get away from it all." Expect to see elk and moose, and maybe even a black bear. Horseback riding, fishing, and hunting are all available. For information and reservations call (800) 303–7256.

JENSEN

Jensen is just a short drive from Vernal, about 20 miles east on two-lane Highway 40. The visitor center here provides maps, brochures, hiking and biking routes as well as rest rooms. Rockhounds will love the **Silver Pick**, a traditional, old-time rock shop. The store is open regular hours during the summer, less often in winter. Here one can choose from bins of rocks and pay for them by the pound. Horseback riding in the area can be booked by calling the **All 'Round Ranch** at (801) 789–7626.

You'll want to save at least a half-day for the next portion of the journey, which includes Dinosaur National Monument and Cub Creek Trail. If it is near lunchtime, consider stopping for food in Vernal (the grocery stores have deli sections, and most of the restaurants will gladly pack lunches), because there is great picnicking to be had in this area. At Jensen's visitor center, look for the Dinosaur Monument sign, and turn left. A winding road takes you to the **Dinosaur Visitor Center and Quarry. Dinosaur National Monument** stretches a hundred miles into Colorado, but the area here is the only place to actually view dinosaur bones. During the summer a shuttle bus operates from the main parking lot; the rest of the year you may drive directly to the quarry building. What you'll find here are four walls and a roof, which literally sit atop one of the most dense fossil discoveries in the world. One hundred and forty-five million years ago this site was a bend in a river, which neatly snagged an accumulation of dead animals. It efficiently buried more than 2,000 bones and the rest, as they say, is history. This find was discovered in the early 1900s by a paleontologist named Earl Douglass. He was exploring the Uinta Basin when he came upon the exposed spine of an apatosaurus. (Can you imagine?) The fossils can still be viewed in their natural state, mostly exposed and lying in their original, 200-foot-long graveyard. During the summer, on the hour, rangers give talks explaining the ongoing excavations in the quarry and out in the field. The quarry also has real dinosaur bones that kids can touch, re-created dinosaurs, and a gift shop that has an excellent selection of dinosaur books as well as coloring books, replicas of petroglyphs, and other cool prehistory items. Call (801) 789–2115 for more information.

Once you've had your fill of dinosaur bones, get back in your car and head out on the **Cub Creek Trail**. It's a left turn out of the parking lot—watch for the numbered signs on the road that indicate Something Significant along the roadside. A helpful printed guide includes a map and descriptions, and may be purchased at the Dinosaur Quarry for fifty cents.

You'll see **Split Mountain**, a mountain effectively divided in two by the Green River. There is a hike here called **Desert Voices Trail**, a 2-mile loop with a long, uphill grade. Split Mountain Campground has picnic tables, but it's exposed to the sun in summer, and is probably too hot for comfort. A short drive down the road to **Green River Campground** provides shadier tables for lunch. You'll pass a boat ramp that is a popular take-out point for river trips, and you may see rafters unpacking their boats here. Continuing on, look for **Turtle Rock** on your left. You'll know it when you see it.

When you reach the dirt road, don't be daunted. In wet weather it can be impassable, but if the road is dry, continuing on from here is worth the effort. Fork left and cross Cub Creek. A bit farther and you'll see superb rock art on your left. This creek and canyon provided safety and a water supply for ancient Indians. At the road's end is the **cabin of Josie Bassett Morris**, a farmer and rancher who took advantage of the same reliable water supply several millenia after the the first inhabitants. Josie Bassett was raised in Brown's Park, lived a long and very full life, and ended her days here, at this wilderness cabin. Her exploits as a cowgirl and adventuress are legendary—she married and divorced five times and reportedly shot one husband, poisoned another, and ran one off while wielding a frying pan. There are rumors, but no proof, that Butch Cassidy was one of her suitors. She settled in Cub Creek in 1914 and built this cabin in 1935 or so. Josie lived here for fifty years, all by herself, and raised pigs, chickens, field crops, and a variety of fruits and vegetables. She had no indoor plumbing or modern conveniences. Next time you're feeling a little blue, remember Josie's remarkable determination.

The nearby trailhead leads 1 mile up **Hog Canyon** and is a nice, easy, one-hour hike. Note: While you're here, stop and listen to the quiet. This corner of the world has no major airplane traffic above, and you're far enough from the highway to escape ground noise.

If your inspection of this area has sparked your family's interest in a river trip, call **Hatch River Expeditions** in Vernal, at (801) 789–4316, and book a trip on the Green River in the Split Mountain Area. For this day-long trip, you will meet your guide in Vernal, at 200 North 400 East, and then take an hour's ride to the put-in spot in Rainbow Park. This is a raucous whitewater trip, with gorgeous canyon scenery along the way. Lunch is included in the fee of $60.00 for adults and $54.00 for children twelve and under. In the spring the water is high and fierce, and children under eight may not participate on this ride. Later in the summer, when the water has gentled, children six and older are welcome.

DUTCH JOHN AND MANILA

Dutch John is a thirty-five-year-old town that literally arose during the course of one year, built by the U.S. Bureau of Reclamation to house the constructors of Flaming Gorge Dam. Manila is home to the Forest Service headquarters for **Flaming Gorge National Recreation Area.** These towns flank **Lake Flaming Gorge**, with Dutch John on the east shore and

Manila near the west. Both are reached by traveling north from Vernal on U.S. Highway 191, and there are several worthwhile stops along the way.

Beginning a few miles out of Vernal, you will see a series of signs that interpret the surrounding geology. Called **Drive Through the Ages**, this road passes over rocks laid down a billion—that's correct, a billion—years ago. You will pass **Steinaker Reservoir State Park**, popular with anglers and water skiers. There is a sandy beach here, along with a self-guided nature trail, rest rooms, a thirty-one-unit campsite, and a water ski slalom course. This water is an important source of irrigation for the valley below. A $3.00 per car day-use fee is charged and camping fees are extra. Call (801) 789-4432 for more information. Continuing on, you will look down at the open pit phosphate mine that has been in operation since 1959.

About 10 miles out of Vernal is **Red Fleet Reservoir State Park**, named for the sailing "fleet" of red rock surrounding the water. Again, fishing and boating are the main activities. There are covered picnic tables, a nice sandy beach, and twenty-nine campsites. A dinosaur trackway dating back 200 million years was recently discovered nearby. Here also, a $3.00 per car day-use fee is charged. More information can be obtained by calling (801) 789-4432. As the road continues its rise, you will head into **Ashley National Forest**. The surroundings turn green and the wildlife is plentiful.

Forty miles outside of Vernal you will meet the junction of Highway 191 and State Route 44. Heading west toward Manila, pull over for a spectacular view at the **Red Canyon Overlook**. This is an excellent choice for a picnic and/or pause-and-reflection. The canyon is 1,500 feet deep. Lake Flaming Gorge spreads out in two directions, with the red slash of rock, for which the gorge is named, providing an electrifying background. There is a forest service visitor center here, and a campground nearby.

If your family wants to continue the quest for really old rocks, you will want to proceed west and take the side road to **Sheep Creek Geological Loop**. This area sustained some very weird earth rotations about two and a half billion years ago, and a drive through here is sort of eerie and fantastical. Today it is called the **Uinta Crest Fault**, and if you look closely you can tell how it was formed: The south side of the fault was thrust up from the earth more than 15,000 feet, while the north side didn't move much at all. The in-between, bent-up parts expose billions of years of geologic history. If you look carefully, you might see the encrusted fossils of sea creatures who lived here when this area was under water.

Continue on to Manila, where motels, restaurants, and a full array of services are waiting. In mid-July the **Cow Country Rodeo** draws visitors from all over the West. On the Saturday night of Labor Day weekend, Manila is famous for its **Festival of Lights.** The celebration begins at dusk, when hundreds of local boaters entertain an onshore crowd by lighting up their boats and traversing in formation on Lake Flaming Gorge. Afterward, a dazzling fireworks display can be seen from the lakeshore. For more information call (800) 477-5558.

From Manila, it is necessary to retrace your route east, back to the junction of State Route 44 and Highway 191. To reach Dutch John, continue northeast on 191. After a short time you will see the signs for the **Oscar Swett Historic Ranch**, and veer left. About a hundred years ago one of the last homesteading projects in the country began here. Oscar Swett and his family used nothing but sweat (no pun intended) and horsepower to create this beautiful ranch, and it is preserved on the National Historic Register as "a vivid example of man learning to live in harmony with nature in order to survive." The ranch is open seasonally, in warm-weather months only. Call (801) 784-3445 for hours and fee information.

A short drive from here leads to the town of Dutch John and **Flaming Gorge Dam**. This is one of the more massive western dam sites, and its sheer bravado as an engineering feat demands notice. The impressive dam rises 502 feet above the mighty Green River, creating Lake Flaming Gorge, which extends 91 miles. Call (801) 784-3445 for visitor information.

The controlled flow of the **Green River** below is excellent for family river-rafting. Half-day trips from just below the dam to **Little Hole** can be booked at **Flaming Gorge Lodge**. The trip costs $175 for up to six people, and you can usually arrange your own departure time. This trip takes about four hours. Call (801) 889-3773 for information. There are a half-dozen river companies in Vernal that will book one- to five-day trips on this river, as well as other rivers in the area. Do-it-yourselfers can rent rafts for self-guided excursions from the Lodge, or from **Flaming Gorge Flying Service** (801-885-3338) and **Flaming Gorge Recreation Services** (801-885-3191).

> **TOP ANNUAL EVENTS FOR THE FAMILY IN NORTHEASTERN UTAH**
>
> Rough Rider Days, June, Roosevelt, (800) 477–5558
> Outlaw Trail Festival, June and July, Vernal, (800) 477–5558
> Dinosaur Round-Up Rodeo, July, Vernal, (800) 477–5558
> Uintah-Ouray Pow Wow, July, Fort Duchesne, (801) 722–5141
> Festival of Lights, August, Manila, (800) 477–5558

Trout fishing is extremely popular here—this stretch of the Green River is oft-cited as one of the premier spots in the world (a trophy mackinaw was taken from the river weighing $51\frac{1}{2}$ pounds). Boaters and fisherpeople flock here year-round, and you will find complete marina facilities, including boat rentals, launching ramps, lodges, and campsites of all comfort levels.

The **Flaming Gorge Dam Visitor Center** is open year-round. Stop here and grab a brochure and fact sheet, and take the self-guided tour of the dam. The tour takes you, via an elevator, into the bowels of the earth. Inside the dam you are surrounded by more tons of concrete than you most likely ever will be again (a million cubic yards), and you are offered a fascinating look at the changes humans can effect on their environment. Guided tours of the dam and special programs for kids are available in the summer. Call (801) 885–3135 for more information.

If your dam experience leaves you in the mood for adventure (and another hour's drive), proceed north on Highway 191 for about 20 miles, until you see the signs for **Brown's Park**. A full gas tank and provisions are advised, because there are no services in Brown's Park. This area is famous as the home to many turn-of-the century eccentrics, who reportedly loved the remoteness here because it kept everybody else away. One of those people was John Jarvie, and his legacy is seen at the **John Jarvie Historic Ranch**, about 20 miles in from Highway 191 (travel is via a dirt road). Jarvie chose this spot because it was an important river crossing, and a hundred years ago he created a resting place for travelers from Utah, Wyoming, and Colorado. His ranch included a store, post office, river ferry, and a reportedly busy cemetery. There was a lot of outlaw activity here in Jarvie's time, and many violent deaths. The area's most famous gunman, Butch Cassidy, was said to do business here, along with his cohort, the Sundance Kid. Jarvie himself was murdered during a robbery at his store. Today the ranch exhibits include an old stone house, a blacksmith shop, and a collection of Western artifacts. Tours of the Jarvie Ranch are conducted May through October, 10:00 A.M. to 5:00 P.M. There is no admission fee. Call (801) 885-3307 for more information.

A **Utah Waterfowl Management Area** is just east of the Jarvie Ranch, and this area is a very popular bird-watching site in the spring and fall.

JONES HOLE

Another fun trip in this region requires a trip back in and out of Vernal, as the road to the **Jones Hole National Fish Hatchery** isn't really on the way to or from anything else. Get on 500 North Street in Vernal, and head east for 40 miles, until just before you reach the Colorado border. Then follow the signs to Jones Hole and Diamond Mountain. You will go up and over **Diamond Mountain** and end up at this little oasis of a place, where people live and work to raise fish for the stocked waters in Utah. There is a visitor center here, bathrooms, picnic tables, and grassy running-around areas. You can go inside the fishery, with its tanks and fish smell, or view the fish outside, from fifty different raceways. Two million fish begin life here each year. Each is one of four different kinds of trout, and most of them are one of five different strains of rainbow. There are no formal tours here, but you can find out everything you need to know, because the nice people who work at the hatchery are very forthcoming with information. If you are in the mood for a walk, consider the trail down to the Green River, which begins near the hatchery raceways. It is 4 miles long, but it's flat, and considered an easy walk. You will see petroglyphs and waterfalls, and if you're extremely lucky, a big horn sheep or two. Call (801) 789-4481 for information on Jones Hole.

Southeastern Utah

This corner of the state is part of a larger area called the Colorado Plateau. *Colorado* is a Spanish word for "red"—and red is definitely the characteristic color of the landscape. Brightly colored sandstone tumbles and falls for hundreds of miles through this country, pausing sometimes to allow a valley oasis to thrive and a town to grow.

The climate differs greatly from northern Utah's alpine terrain. Winters here are mild, making outdoor sports popular all year long. Mountain bikers have made this area their mecca, hiking and backpacking are spectacular, and river running is a major industry—on both the thrilling rapids of the Green and Colorado rivers and the tamer waters of the languid San Juan River.

There are many sacred Native American sites here, both ancient and modern, and incredible rock-art panels. Enjoy the beauty of two national parks as well as Lake Powell and Rainbow Bridge National Monument. Monument Valley, made famous in dozens of Western movies, guards the southern border.

MOAB

For its first half-century of settlement, Moab was a quiet, dusty town, pretty much in the middle of nowhere. That changed dramatically in the 1950s, when huge uranium deposits were discovered in the area. Moab became the center of a booming mining industry that drew thousands of hopeful prospectors. Much money was made and lost, but the most last-

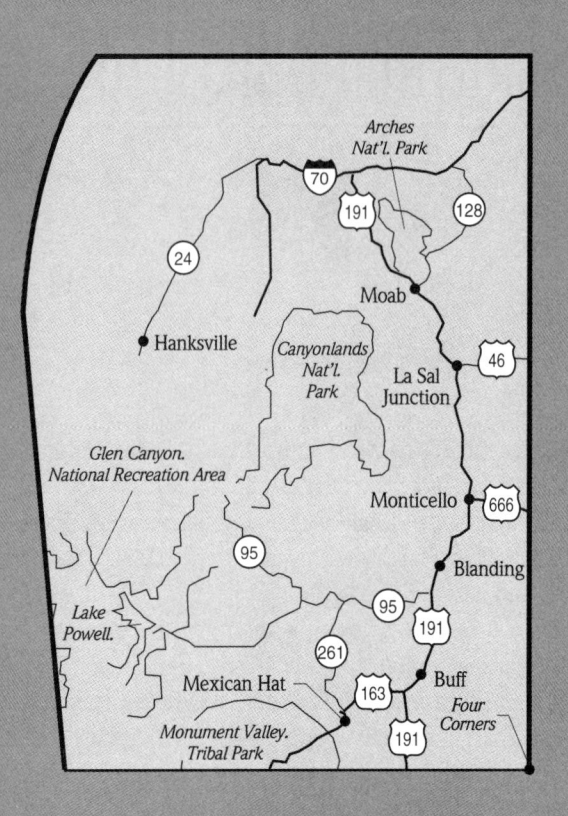

Southeastern Utah

ing effect was that Moab was "discovered"—and has never been the same since.

The town is now a bustling activity center for the tourist trade. Thousands of vacationers flock here to enjoy the scenic and recreational beauty nearby.

A good first stop is the **Moab Information Center**, on the corner of Center and Main. The nice people here can help you with directions as well as restaurant and lodging selections. They also know about evening activities and seasonal goings-on. Great maps and a selection of books describing the area are for sale. Call (801) 259–8825 for more information.

Shopping is a pleasant diversion in Moab's bustling downtown area. The **jewelry shops on Main Street** make for great browsing and buying. Look for silver jewelry hand-crafted by Utah Indians and decorated with native rock such as turquoise and topaz. The bookstores in town have good selections of natural history and western geology books; local art galleries feature unique Native American sculpture and paintings; rock collectors will find a great selection here. A couple of fun shops are **Marc II** and the **Trading Post**, where your children will find clever toys, gadgets, and collectibles. Both of these stores are located in a small mall on Main Street and 50 South, next to a popular brew pub called **Eddie McStiffs**. Note: Children can eat in the restaurant adjoining the brew pub but are not allowed in the bar.

The **Dan O'Laurie Canyon Country Museum**, at 118 East Center, interprets the history and prehistory of both man and beast who lived in this area. The Pierson History Hall traces the development of ranching, early transportation, and the Old Spanish Trail. The museum is named after its modern-day benefactor. The museum is open six days a week, and hours vary with the seasons. There is no admission fee, however a donation is greatly appreciated. For more information, call (801) 259–7985.

The **Butch Cassidy Water Slide** is a good way to cool off in Moab. Open during the summer season, the winding tubes and open slides here are very popular with pre-teens. No other water park in the world can boast King World, a weird, very old carving, done in stone, that sits a few hundred feet above the water activity. King World was named by its now-forgotten sculptor, and features a king's head and a horse's head. If you want a close-up look at this oddity, ask and a guide will accompany you to the site. The water park takes its name from the original natural pond located here, which was a reported watering hole for the outlaw Butch Cassidy. In season, the park is open seven days a week. Full-day passes are less than $10. Call (801) 259–2837 for more information. Another fun place for kids is **Ya Gotta Wanna Fun Park**, located behind McDonald's on Kane Creek Boulevard. Mini golf, paddle boats, and a go-cart track will entertain the older children in your family. Call (801) 259–8007 for admission and park hours.

While you're in this part of the world, you'll often notice the beautiful **LaSal Mountains** looming in the background. This range is the headland for part of the Manti-LaSal National Forest. Its green, snow-capped peaks are a much-photographed scenic contrast to the red rock of the lowlands. The LaSals are a getaway spot for those looking for relief from the summer heat. Excellent fishing is found here in dozens of streams and lakes. A favorite spot for children is **Oowah Lake**, found by driving Highway 191 twelve miles south of town and following the signs for the Scenic Loop road. Once on the Scenic Loop road, it's another 28 miles to the lake. In winter, **Geyser Pass** is a favorite place with families for sledding, snowmobiling, and cross-country skiing. To find the pass, follow Highway 191 south of town until the Pack Creek cut-off, and then follow the Scenic Loop road to the signed turn-off. Geyser Pass has miles of groomed trails that branch from its trailhead; ask locally for a route that will fit your skiing ability.

The LaSals are one reigning natural force in southeastern Utah; another is the **Colorado River.** The Colorado may look fairly tame as it runs through town, but a few miles north and south are wild, whitewater canyons famous for rafting. Moab is the put-in point for a dozen rafting companies that take adventurers on both calm water and whitewater trips on the Colorado and Green rivers, which join together just south of town. If you're a novice, it's highly recommended that you book with a guide for this experience. **North American** (801) 259–5865, **Navtech** (801) 259–7983, and **Tag-A-Long** (801) 259–8946 are among the many rafting outfits in town that cater to families. They offer shorter trips for small children; older children can ride along on anything from half-day to multiple-day trips. Be aware that in spring the water is high and fast, and often children under eight are not allowed on the river. Later in the year, when the water is tamer, children over six may join the fun. A typical guided trip involves a boat guide who is thoroughly acquainted with the rapids and the history and the geology of the area, an inflated rubber raft that holds between eight and ten rafters, and oars and life jackets for everybody. Expect to pay about $30 per person for a half-day trip.

A river and camping trip designed just for families is offered by **Sheri Griffith Expeditions**. Called **Coyote Run**, the two-day, one-night trip takes children as young as four years old down a mild stretch of the Colorado River in paddleboats and inflatable kayaks. At night you'll camp at old ranch homestead on the riverbank, and, if you're willing, you can sleep in an authentic reproduction of a Sioux Indian tepee. Dinner is cooked by your river guide in Dutch ovens over an open campfire. This outing is meant to recreate life along the river as it was at the turn of the century—except with less work and a lot more fun. A similar but longer trip is offered on the Green River. For prices, dates, and more information, call (800) 332-2439.

Dry land activities in this area are popular as well. Bicycling has been made famous in Moab by the **Slickrock Trail,** perhaps the best-known fat-tire route in the country. This is a difficult trail, with the only guide an occasional slash of paint on the rock, requiring about five hours for completion of its loop. The Slickrock Trail is noteworthy for its thrilling ups and downs over colorful sandstone, especially lovely at sunset or sunrise. If you and your family are not seasoned bikers, you might want to try the 2.3-mile "practice loop" located nearby. Another good family ride is to the top of **Hurrah Pass**; head out on Kane Creek Road until you reach a graded dirt road, then it's about another 3 miles to the top, climbing two hills along the way. The annual **Fat Tire Festival**, always the week of Halloween, features fun family rides and activities. For more information, call (801) 375-3231.

There are many family hikes with trailheads in and around Moab. Children will love the 3-mile round trip to **Corona Arch**, which involves steps cut into the rock and a ladder. This trail begins 10 miles west of the junction of Highways 279 and 191, from a parking lot on the north side of the highway. Another good bet is the hike to **Millcreek Canyon's** waterfall, a mile-and-a-half round trip that involves wading through several streams. This trail begins at the end of Power House Lane, in the southeastern part of Moab. For more hiking information, pick up a "Hiking Trails" brochure at the visitor center.

The spectacular scenery in and around Moab has provided the backdrop for many movies, from *Rio Grande*, made in 1950 and starring John Wayne, to *Thelma and Louise*, made in 1992. Many of these **movie locations** can be visited, and some have sets that have remained after the Hollywood crews have returned home. Pick up a "Movie Locations Auto Tour" brochure at the visitor center, and show the cinema buffs in your family where more than a dozen movies were filmed.

About 2 miles north of Moab on Highway 191, you will see the turn-off to Highway 128 and the **Colorado River Scenic Byway**. This is a gorgeous road, and your family will enjoy the great hiking and sightseeing along the way. The road travels 44 miles and requires about two hours to travel to its terminus, Cisco, and back. Notable features on the byway are **Big Bend Picnic Area**, with its wide, sandy beach on the Colorado River; **Castle Valley Junction**, with a view of Castle Rock, an improbable, slender monolith of stone made famous in rock music videos and car commercials; the crumbling flanks of **Fisher Towers**, with a picnic area and hiking trails; and the historic **Dewey Suspension Bridge,** built in 1916 and used until 1986 and listed on the National Register of Historic Places.

You may have viewed some spectacular red-rock formations in Utah, but until you have been to **Arches National Park** you have not seen 2,000 stone openings spanning their way across a 73,000-acre protected reserve. Your family is in for a treat! The arches are everywhere, great big ones and little tiny ones, interspersed with wonderful rock spires and turrets and monoliths. It's recommended that you leave at least a half-day for this adventure, and bring along a picnic lunch. Every family member should have plenty of portable water to take along on the many hikes in the park. For advance information on Arches and its amenities, call (801) 259–8161, or write Arches National Park, P.O. Box 907, Moab 84532. To get to Arches, travel 4½ miles north from Moab on U.S. Highway 191 until you see the turn-off sign. Pay your $4.00 fee, which is good for seven days. Then look immediately to your right, spot the Visitor Center, park

> **MARGARET'S TOP FAMILY ADVENTURES IN SOUTHEASTERN UTAH**
>
> 1. Rafting on the Colorado, Green and San Juan rivers
> 2. Arches National Park
> 3. Island In The Sky (Canyonlands National Park)
> 4. Hovenweep National Monument
> 5. Driving the Moki Dugway

your car, and head in. There are friendly rangers here and all sorts of good orientation information.

If you want to hike the **Fiery Furnace** (this is a terrific family hike and highly recommended, even if you have to come back on another day), now is the time to sign up for this unforgettable only-with-a-ranger guided expedition. Look at the pictures that describe the plant and animal life you'll see here. It's amazing to discover the variety of life that manages to thrive in this high desert country. Take time to study the geology tables. The sandstone all over this region was laid down in different geologic eras, and each one has a name and a history. There are many unique formations here—on your drive through the park see if you can spot *The Penguins*, *Sausage Rock*, *Three Gossips*, and *Adam and Eve*.

Now you are ready to hit the park's 41-mile loop road. Wind around for a mile to **Park Avenue**, the first stopping spot. The main feature here is the vertical slab on your right, which forms a huge "storefront" to the "avenue." Strolling down the avenue is an easy mile if you arrange to get picked up at North Park Avenue. The next stop is another 1½ miles up the road, at **Courthouse Towers**. These monoliths were probably arches at one time. The largest is called **Sheep Rock**, and you can see the "sheep" looking longingly across a breach to their sandstone grazing grounds. Look just to the left for **Baby Arch**, and you will have a lesson in how arches are formed. On to **Petrified Dunes**, which, in fact, were real sand dunes a couple of million years ago. You will notice the rock's whiter color here—this is Navajo sandstone, which contains a smaller amount of the iron that colors the rocks nearby. About 9 miles from the Visitor Center is **Balanced Rock**—a perfect example of two varieties of sandstone, with different hardening agents, at work against the elements. A huge boulder (about 3,500 tons) sits on top of a smaller boulder, performing one of nature's more precarious balancing acts. This is a good spot to take pictures of the red rock with the green LaSal Mountains courteously making a perfect backdrop.

A short drive down the road brings you to **The Windows** section of the park; if your family enjoys hiking, you'll want to get out of the car and walk around for an hour or so. Remind your family that nature really did make these arches—they are so whimsical and perfect that it seems Disney might have had something to do with it instead. **North and South Windows** are so named because both arches provide a perfect frame for the gorgeous scenery beyond. These are two arches formed inside the same huge fin, and if you face them directly but back up a couple hundred feet, you will see why they are also known as **The Spectacles** (as in eyeglasses, not public embarrassments). **Turret Arch** is just across the way, with its castle-like capstone.

Back in the car, drive just a few minutes on, to **Double Arch**. This requires an easy five-minute walk to see its twin image. These arches were formed differently—see if you can tell which was originally a pothole, and which was formed by water and wind beating against its rock fin. Stand at the end of the trail, and you can see the **Parade of Elephants,** leading a billion-year-old circus march. Less than 2 miles beyond is **Pothole Arch**, so named because water that once rushed down from above formed a depression in the rock, which after an inconceivable amount of time formed a hole in the cliff side, which after another very long time wore away to leave only this span of stone.

Hang on. The next stop is The Big One. **Delicate Arch** is an extraordinary formation. It has become Utah's signature arch, celebrated on license plates and official road signs. You can see Delicate from a roadside turn-out, but this is a must-see-close-up kind of thing, and its 3-mile round-trip hike is worth the effort. If your children hike this trail in the full heat of summer, you will need a lot of water and rest stops. If you visit the area during the cooler months, the hike seems easier and you will need less hydration. Be warned that you are exposed to the full sun for much of this hike, it's a 500-foot elevation rise, and it's officially labeled "moderately strenuous"—so plan accordingly. Just past the trailhead to Delicate are the remains of **Wolfe Ranch**, where a hardy family lived for twenty years at the turn of the century. Take a moment to marvel at the hardships they must have faced.

Shortly on, you'll reach a sandy path, then cross a bouncy bridge. Just past the bridge, look for a side trail on your left. Follow this around the corner for about a hundred yards and you'll see a large **Ute Indian petroglyph panel**. Continuing on, after the switchbacks, the boulder portion of the hike is the most strenuous, as it climbs over rolling slickrock marked by rock cairns. Nature provides suspense as you near the arch, hiding it from view until the very end. When you turn the final bend—voila!—a 45-foot arch inside a sandstone bowl the size of a small town, gleefully teetering on sandstone high heels. A natural stone bench provides an excellent view, and if you're feeling brave, you can hike into the slippery bowl and actually stand under the arch. Like every good thing, Delicate has been discovered by the hordes, but if you are lucky and see it on an uncrowded day (which probably will not happen in the summer), it is unbeatable as a picnic/contemplation spot.

Back in the car, the next pull-out point is **Fiery Furnace**, but you will notice this intense cluster of rock flame-fins before you get there. The Furnace is so winding and convoluted that a ranger's accompaniment is needed, which requires a sign-up at the visitor center, and often at least a day's notice. This is an especially great expedition for kids—all sorts of squeezing through narrow places and jumping-off things and poisonous plant sitings. The naming of the Fiery Furnace is an obvious choice, but if you see this formation at sunset, you will view it in its fullest, flaming beauty. Next up is **Sand Dune Arch**. Small kids love the 30-yard walk to this arch, because it requires squeezing between two rock fins to see it. Nature has made a terrific sandpile here, and this place is shady for most of the day. If you feel like walking further, you will come to **Broken Arch**, named because it looks broken from a distance (it really isn't).

Another mile up the road you will pass **Skyline Arch**, on your way to the third, and final, big hike of the day, in **Devil's Garden**. The hike in Devil's Garden can be split up a number of ways. The main trail will take you to **Pine Tree Arch** (a short side trip and well-signed—when you get to the "T" in this trail, go right for a view of **Tunnel Arch**, left to Pine Tree), **Landscape, Navajo, Partition, Double O,** and **Dark Angel arches**. If you make it all the way to Dark Angel you deserve a merit badge. The length is not prohibitive—7.2 miles round trip—but you are walking in sand for much of the way, and after **Landscape Arch** the trail gets iffy as you are following cairns, and it is just plain tiring. The most popular destination is Landscape Arch—about a mile in from the trailhead on a well-marked path. Landscape is the longest known natural span in the world, with an inside width of 306 feet. You can hike up the short side trail to Landscape, sit under it, and contemplate man's small place in the universe. The very apparent land restoration going on here is an educational lesson in what it takes to save an area from being "loved to death."

Near the Devil's Garden parking lot, you will see the **Devil's Garden Campground**. It has fifty-two beautiful sites, many of them clustered with juniper and bordered by big mounds of sandstone. From March through October, weather permitting, the campground has running water, and the nightly fee is $8.00. During the colder weather months water is not available in the campground (bring your own or else fill up at the visitor center) and the nightly fee is $5.00. Advance reservations are not taken; these campsites must be registered for at the visitor center the day of your arrival. Be aware that this is the only camping possibility in the park, and it is nearly always full. There are many privately owned campgrounds within ten miles of Arches. For information on private campgrounds and other lodging possibilities, call (800) 635–MOAB. After an hour or two at Devil's Garden, it's an 18-mile drive back to the Visitor Center. Activities at Arches include campfire chats every night of the week during the summer. Topics include "Why scorpions live in the parks," "Shaman's paint box," and "Why Arches?"

Another Very Big Deal near Moab is **Canyonlands National Park**, a park so big it's been split into three very distinct sections: the Maze, the Needles, and Island in the Sky. These areas adjoin each other but are neatly trisected by the Colorado and Green rivers and must be reached from different entry points. A fourth section of the park, Horseshoe Canyon, is reached by yet another road. Canyonlands' vast expanse dwarfs Arches National Park and makes Arches, with its paved roads and signed trails, seem almost tame. This is not the place to fool around with Mother Nature. Get directions, have provisions on hand, and be careful. For information, write Canyonlands National Park, 125 West 200 South, Moab 84532, or call (801) 259-7164.

The Maze is reached from Utah Highways 24 or 95 and is passable only in a four-wheel-drive vehicle or on a mountain bike. The Maze is known as one of the most remote places on earth—not in terms of distance but in terms of how-many-tons-of-sandstone-between-you-and-others. Once you enter this 30-square-mile tangle of rock wilderness you'll truly be away from it all. If you're extremely hardy, you might make it all the way to the **Doll's House**, 40 miles in on a dirt road. You'll be rewarded with an incredible surround of colorful rock formations, and a stunning view downward of the Colorado River.

The Needles section is more family-friendly. Named for its predominant red-rock spires, the Needles is about an hour-and-a-half drive from Moab. To get here, travel 50 miles south of Moab on Highway 191, and turn right onto Highway 211 at the CANYONLANDS NATIONAL PARK road sign. Note: You will pass a turn-off for BLM's Needles Overlook Road. About 20 miles in on this road you'll pass **Newspaper Rock**—a great introduction to rock art for kids, and a very worthwhile stop. From prehistory through frontier days, people felt the need to make their mark here, and the result is a crowded mix of messages on a huge rock wall. Perhaps it was the black oxide surface of this rock, which makes carving through it easy and distinct, or perhaps it was its location as an ancient trail—but for whatever reasons, Newspaper Rock is an amazing amalgam of history.

Moving on, it is about 25 more miles to The Needles themselves. The park service has thoughtfully put a **visitor center** here, because you will probably need directions and a bathroom. Here, your family is treated to a view of artifacts, displays, a short film, and a book shop. The park entrance fee is $4.00 per vehicle and is good for seven days. **Squaw Flats Campground** and its wonderful sites are nearby, however they are first-come, first-served, and the campground fills up most summer nights. Running water is available here during the warm weather months; in winter you are asked to bring your own. There is a $6.00 overnight fee. For more information on camping at Squaw Flats, call the park's main information number at (801) 259-7164. Picnic tables in the campground and at the visitor center are pleasant for lunch, although with all the wildness surrounding you, your family might prefer a more remote spot down the road.

Back on the road, look for **The Wooden Shoe** formation—when you spot it, you will definitely know what you're looking at. Two excellent family hikes in this area are recommended. **Roadside Ruin** is a short, easy, loop trail. Pick up the interpretive pamphlet for this hike at the visitor center, so you can identify the flora and fauna along the way. This area was occupied by Indians a century ago who used this same flora and fauna for sustenance. One of their better-preserved storage houses constitutes the "ruin" of this hike. Just down the road is the pull-out parking area for the **Cave Spring Trail**, a .6-mile loop. This hike involves lots of fun things including climbing two ladders, viewing an old cowboy camp, and finding Indian markings on boulders. If you are prepared with a four-wheel-drive vehicle, continue on the Cave Spring dirt road to **Paul Bunyan's Potty,** the fodder for many grade-school jokes. This giant rock formation could be described, but you probably get the idea.

The BIG things in The Needles are **Chesler Park**, the **confluence of the Green and Colorado rivers**, and **Angel Arch**. However, all three of these natural phenomena require not just a four-wheel-drive vehicle, but an experienced driver. The roads are classified for difficulty, and they are all pretty high up on the scale. The trade-off is that this area provides high adventure and solitude. Ask a ranger before you head out on any of these potentially dangerous roads. Chesler Park is a huge, scrub-grass meadow rimmed by the needle-shaped rock for which this park is named. In Chesler you get your best sense of how the needles were formed, and of their size and shape. To view the confluence of the Green and Colorado rivers, follow the road to the Big Spring Canyon Overlook, and then set out on dirt for a hefty four-wheel drive. Park at the sign and hike the last mile or so of this trail. When you reach the terminus, you're rewarded with a heart-stopping view, straight down, of the joining of these two mighty rivers. As mentioned at the beginning of this chapter, *Colorado* is a Spanish word for "red," you know what green is, and the rivers are actually green and red. When they join, they turn a third, marvelous, color. This is not for the vertigo-impaired. You'll probably see pictures of Angel Arch in the visitor center. Again, this trail follows a long four-wheel-drive route into Salt Creek Canyon (it's a lot of fun if you're equipped), and requires a strenuous hike. But this 150-foot-high winged arch is simply breathtaking.

A vivid contrast to The Needles and The Maze, **Island in the Sky** is not about rock scrambling, hidden picnic spots, or dirt roads. This lofty perch offers sweeping mesas and an eagle's-eye view of the world. Bonus—the road is paved almost the entire way! The entrance to the Island is on Highway 313, reached by heading north on U.S. Highway 191 from Moab. The **Visitor Center** at Island in the Sky is open all year from 8:00 A.M. to 5:00 P.M. in summer, and from 8:00 A.M. to 4:30 P.M. in winter. There are rest rooms and a drinking fountain here, as well as a bookstore and a theater showing films that describe the area. Note: It is recommended that you bring plenty of water along on your visit; there are no water stations on Island in the Sky. The $4.00 entrance fee to the park is good for seven days.

After a short drive out onto this section of the park it becomes apparent how the Island got its name. This high peninsula towers above the winding rivers below, offering fabulous viewpoints from the pull-outs that dot its scenic route. You'll see canyon after canyon rolling into the far distance. Three mountain ranges rim the horizon   they catch all of the water that would fall here, which is one reason why the mountains are blue-green in the distance but the closer view is of barren red rock. The **Henry Mountains** are to the southwest, the **Abajos** (a Navajo word for "blue") are to the south, and the **LaSals** are to the east. The closest mesa you'll see is the massive **White Rim**, which runs almost continuously below the Island. You'll also view both The Needles and The Maze from this elevated point in space.

There are a couple of easy hikes on the Island. The **Mesa Arch Trail** is a short route looping across a piñon and juniper plain to the edge of the mesa. The arch here is a perfect frame for the LaSal Mountains in the distance. Pick up a guide to the geology and plant life of this trail at the visitor center. The **Upheaval Dome Crater View Trail** leads just 500 yards to the remains of an incredibly turbulent geologic event. Tons of layers of rock were pushed up, and others fell down—and the result is a big bowl of . . . rock. Your family will enjoy this dome because its scope is small enough that kids can grasp its geologic significance. Again, a pamphlet can be found at the visitor center explaining just exactly what happened here. **Buck Canyon Overlook** and **Grand View Point Overlook** complete the scenic drive.

Horseshoe Canyon, a non-adjoining section of the park, is federally designated to protect its rare rock art. Horseshoe is a magical place, but entrance to the canyon requires a bumpy ride on a dirt road and then a strenuous hike—straight down a cliff side, with much of the trail in deep sand. The return, of course, is straight up a cliff side in deep sand. The canyon is reached via Utah Highway 24, and is more easily accessed from the town of Green River than from Moab. The destination in Horseshoe is **The Grand Gallery**—a bigger-than-life–sized ancient drawing of fifty figures, stretching for more than 80 feet along the canyon wall. Perhaps because of its isolated location, the rock art has not been disturbed by humans for the last 2,000 years or so. A walk through this canyon evokes the magic and mystery that were integral to the Indians who lived here so long ago.

Throughout Canyonlands National Park backcountry camping, accessed by backpackers and four-wheelers, is allowed. Reservations and permits for this type of camping must be arranged at park visitor centers or by calling (801) 259–4351. A backpacking permit costs $10.00, a four-wheel permit costs $25.00, and both are good for seven days.

On the road to Island in the Sky on Highway 313, you will pass the turn-off to one of Utah's premier parks, **Dead Horse Point State Park**. The perfect time to reach Dead Horse is just as the sun is starting to think about setting. You can take the short walk to the overlook and sit and relax and let the 1,000-mile view out there sear itself into your consciousness. But beware, there are all sorts of ways to fall off a cliff here—don't discover any of them. Dead Horse is a narrow, high mesa jutting out into heaven atop cliffs called the **Orange Escarpment.** It is not named after a bunch of horses who jumped off these cliffs. It seems a few generations ago this spot was used as a corral because it required a minimum of fencing, the cliffs providing an effective barrier for horses. One story tells of an errant cowboy who penned up a herd of horses and then apparently forgot about them. When the poor beasts were discovered, they had died of thirst, probably looking longingly down the 2,000-foot cliffs at the rushing waters of the Colorado River. Speaking of the Colorado, it takes a very show-offy turn just below Dead Horse Point. One of its better goosenecks performs in perpetuity right in front of your eyes. Try to figure out which way the flow goes. Dead Horse Point State Park has an entrance fee of $3.00 per vehicle. Camping is $8.00 per night, and reservations may be made by calling (800) 322–3770 at least three days in advance. Campers are asked to bring their own water. There is a visitor center, pavilion, and large overlook shelter from which to absorb the view. For more information, write Dead Horse Point State Park, P.O. Box 609, Moab 84532–0609, or call (801) 259–2614.

If you seek a bird's-eye view of southeastern Utah, you're in luck. **Scenic Aviation** (801–678–3222) in Blanding and **Midway Aviation** (801–587–2774) offer aerial tours of all of the parks, and just about anything else you'd like to see in this part of the world.

LASAL JUNCTION

The services in this tiny berg consist of a post office and a mini-mart. But about 5 miles north, on Highway 191, is a truly unique attraction known as **Hole 'N the Rock**. Fifty years ago, this was just a rock (without 'n hole). Then along came a sculptor named Christensen, who saw some potential, and began blasting away to create the present site. This was the Christensen family's home for many years, and now the original owners are buried nearby. Today Hole 'N the Rock is a gift shop, snack bar, and American original.

Just a few miles south of LaSal Junction, on Highway 191, are **Looking Glass Rock** and **Wilson Arch**. Looking Glass requires a 1-mile drive on a dirt road to see its large, round opening-in-a-rock. Wilson, another big hole, is just off the road. A bit farther on, to the west, you'll see the turn-off to **Canyon Rims Recreation Area**. This is a 22-mile, paved road that skims along a narrow, mile-high peninsula with powerful vistas all around. The terminus is **Needles Overlook**, a picnic tabled–area, where you'll look down into Canyonlands National Park. Do take time to stop at **Anticline Overlook**, one of the more fabulous lookout points in the state. Picnic tables, interpretive displays, and hiking trails are located here.

MONTICELLO

This bustling town sits on the edge of the Manti–La Sal National Forest and takes its green scenery and cooler climate from the nearby mountains. Yes, it's named after Thomas Jefferson's home, but in Utah it is pronounced Mon-ti-*s*ello. A casual restaurant in town with a great children's meu is **MD Ranchhouse,** found on South Main Street. Cal (801) 587–3299. The **Monticello Museum** is located inside the city library, with Indian and pioneer artifacts and rocks. The **San Juan County Travel Council** is located at 117 South Main, ready and waiting with books, brochures, and maps that interpret the area. For information, call (801) 587–3235.

BLANDING

A serendipitous circumstance has left Blanding with a wonderful **Dinosaur Museum,** at 754 South 200 West. It seems a family of paleontologists with a private collection of fossils fell in love with the area and decided to live here. A suitable building to house the collection became available and—voila! a world-class museum. Several of the displays here don't exist anywhere else, including rare petrified wood and ancient fossils. There are lots of little cases with neat displays, and dioramas that explain ancient life. Real-life dinosaur bones have been pieced together to their original state. One of the dinosaur builders is a skin specialist and believes that dinosaurs were very brightly colored. You'll see his work on display. The museum is open from mid-April to mid-October, Monday through Saturday from 8:00 A.M. to 5:00 P.M. Admission is $2.00 for adults and $1.00 for children. Call (801) 678–3454 for more information.

Shopping for handmade Indian crafts is rewarding here. **Huck's Museum and Trading Post,** ½ mile south of town on Highway 191, (801) 678–2329, has a large display of Indian artifacts and a shop that sells Navajo-crafted gifts. **Cedar Mesa Pottery,** at 333 South Main (801) 678–2241, sells handmade pottery, and during the week you can watch the potters ply their craft in the factory next door. The **Blue Mountain Trading Post,** just south of town on Highway 191, (801) 678–2218, has a big selection of jewelry, art, and kachina dolls.

In a residential neighborhood in Blanding is **Edge of the Cedars State Park**. Follow the signs from Main Street around lots of corners, and just when you're sure you're lost, there it is. This park is dedicated to the ancient inhabitants of this neighborhood and features the remains of an Anasazi Indian pueblo and its ceremonial kivas. The Anasazis, also called "the ancient ones," flourished in southeastern Utah between 700 and 1220 A.D. They irrigated and grew crops and raised livestock. Then, suddenly, their population vanished, and nobody knows why. The Edge of the Cedars Museum has collections of artifacts and pottery, and the only known metal Anasazi artifacts in Utah. Navajo, Ute, and early Anglo cultures are interpreted as well. Call (801) 678–2338 for more information.

You can get take-out at several of Blanding's restaurants, including pizza and pasta at **The Cedar Pony** at 191 North Highway 191 and burgers at the **Patio Drive-In** at 95 North Highway 191. Armed with food, find the park and tables in the center of town, or else enjoy the nice picnic area at Edge of the Cedars State Park. For information about Blanding, write to P.O. Box 490, 117 South Main Street, Blanding 84535, or call (801) 587–3235.

BLUFF

This beautiful oasis was settled in the late 1800s by Mormon pioneers and was the first Anglo town in this quarter of the state. The pioneers had been directed by Mormon Church leaders to explore and settle this area and to establish friendly relations with the local Indians. The story of their journey south from Salt Lake City is one of horrific hardships and sacrifice. Their painful legacy is literally etched in stone at **Hole-in-the-Rock** (which can be seen by traveling to the town of Escalante, heading 5 miles east of town, and then heading south on a rugged dirt road for 60 miles). This "hole" is a small break in the sheer cliffs of Glen Canyon, with a drop into Lake Powell. The rugged pioneers pushed their wagons and cattle through the hole and lowered them by rope to the water, where they then ferried their possessions across to dry land. This labor took months longer than the pioneers had planned for the trip. Their destination was about 15 miles east of Bluff, at Montezuma Creek. But by the time the settlers arrived at Bluff they were too exhausted to continue. This proved to be fortuitous, as Bluff, with its artesian wells, proved to be a more hospitable environment.

Today the entire town of Bluff is designated as an historic district. The main road through town doesn't really show off Bluff's history. Turn west onto any side road and you'll be treated to wide, shady streets lined with original pioneer homes. Look for the **Jens Nielson House** as one fine example of pioneer enterprise. You'll notice right away that farming is an important industry here. You'll notice soon after that river running is also of economic importance to the town. A major put-in point for rafters on the San Juan River, **Sand Island,** is just a few minutes west of town.

This is major silver-jewelry-buying country. You're on the northern tip of a huge Navajo Indian reservation, and there is evidence everywhere of that rich cultural influence. Look for beautiful workmanship and great buys. **Twin Rocks Trading Post,** on the north end of town on Highway 191, named for the **Navajo Twins** rock formation nearby, has a big selection of Navajo and Zuni jewelry, belt buckles, hair fasteners, and other good stuff. Across the street, **Cow Canyon Trading Post and Restaurant** sells wonderfully small, handmade, clay farm animals and figurines, and there are beautiful rugs and fabric bolts here as well as good food. If you've never had a Navajo taco, run, don't walk, to the **Sunbonnet Cafe,** found on the Historic Loop. Also, take time to visit **St. Christopher's Episcopal Mission,** established by a hardworking priest more than fifty years ago. Find the mission by heading east from town on Highway 163 for about a mile. About 2 miles farther on from the mission is a **swinging bridge,** which is fun to walk across. It was used by children from the reservation for access to school in town. The cemetery on the hill provides a great view and some local history.

In May, Bluff hosts **Head Start Days**, a child-centered celebration with a parade, concessions, and Indian dances. If you're in town in early June, ask about the annual **Indian Day Celebration**, a festival of games, good food, and horse races. The first weekend in September brings the **White Mesa Ute Council Bear Dance,** a three-day affair featuring contests, a cook-out, games, and, of course, native dances. In mid-September Bluff hosts the **Utah Navajo Fair**, with a rodeo and pow wow. For information on events in Bluff, call (801) 587–3235.

Lodging here is not plentiful, so book ahead. **Recapture Lodge** is a good bet, with a helpful staff, historic surroundings, and evening lectures—try to stay upstairs where the surrounding deck offers a shady spot at day's end. For reservations call (801) 672–2281.

A river trip in this part of the world is highly recommended. The **San Juan River** is user-friendly (although rapids do exist—don't be fooled by first impressions!) and perfect for those who aren't ready for the thrills of whitewater. Two popular trips depart from near Bluff—put-in at Sand Island and take out at **Mexican Hat,** and/or put-in at Mexican Hat and take out at **Clay Hills.** If you go to Sand Island, find the rock panel that displays the five ancient images of Kokopelli—easily distinguished by his humpback and flute. Kokopelli is a popular Hopi Indian legendary figure, who among other things, could supposedly stop winter weather with his flute. An outfitter in Bluff called **Wild Rivers Expeditions** takes families on one– to seven-day trips on the San Juan. Call (801) 672–2244 for more information.

There are also many easy, scenic bike trails near Bluff. One of the best is in **Valley of the Gods**, located west of Bluff, off Highway 163. Valley of the Gods is a 27-mile loop trail; pedal just a few miles in and out, and you'll find a level road and lots of good scenery. The valley is named for its stately stone formations—you'll see empirical monoliths and mighty beasts. The predominant butte at the start of the trail is 400-foot-high **Seven Sailors.**

From Bluff, take Highway 191 north to the intersection of Highway 262, turn right, and follow the signs to the **Hatch Trading Post**. If you want to see a traditional Indian trading post, stop here. This is the equivalent of a corner grocery for the Navajo tribe.

Farther on down the road is **Hovenweep National Monument**, an exceptionally well-preserved ancient Indian city, with 20-foot-high tower walls still standing, generally agreed to be at least 700 years old. From the parking lot you'll approach the most accessible ruins, a grouping called **Square Tower**. Square Tower is one of six groups of ruins at Hovenweep. Trails emanating from here include three short loop trails that total about 1½ miles. This is an easy cairn-led hike, perfect for small children if the weather cooperates—it gets VERY hot here in summer. Borrow a trail-guide pamphlet at the ranger station, or buy one for fifty cents. As you're walking through this place, remember that these towers and rooms were built about the same time as the medieval castles in Europe. A network of dirt roads connects the five outlying ruin groups. There is a ranger station and visitor center here, a campground that is sometimes closed, rest rooms, and bottled drinking water. There is no admission fee. For more information about Hovenweep National Monument call (970) 529-4461.

LAKE POWELL

Look at any list of Utah's most popular tourist attractions, and you'll see Temple Square in Salt Lake City at the top of the list, and **Glen Canyon National Recreation Area** a close second. Tourists love this boating mecca for its warm, blue water and steep, red rock cliff surround.

Glen Canyon is a million-acre, federally-owned expanse of land stretching from Canyonlands National Park, across the southern border of Utah, and down into Grand Canyon National Park in Arizona. The government's purpose here, besides providing recreation for three million people every year, is to control the flow of the Colorado River in order to supply water and electricity to the surrounding states of Arizona, New Mexico, Nevada, and California. This was accomplished first in 1963, with the completion of Glen Canyon Dam. Before the dam, Glen Canyon was a steep, many tributaried, tangle of red rock. Today visitors "float" above the canyon floor, about half way up the side of the old rocks. When you're on the lake, think about the grottoes, natural arches, and Indian artifacts below you. Before, during and after the dam was built many people objected to its invasion of environmentally sensitive landscapes. Several attempts to halt construction have since become legendary. For a fictionalized account this time and place, read *The Monkey Wrench Gang* by western author Eward Abbey.

Drive west from Blanding on State Route 95, and veer south onto State Route 276. A two-hour drive from here will deposit you on the shores of **Lake Powell**, the reservoir that has backed up behind Glen Canyon Dam and the central recreation area of Glen Canyon. Powell takes its name from John Wesley Powell, the intrepid explorer who first charted these waters in 1869. You'll see monuments and plaques documenting his journey all over the place.

Lake Powell has one of the more convoluted shorelines on the planet. The lake is 186 miles long, with almost 2,000 miles of shoreline. You read correctly—that's a shoreline more than ten times as long as its length. For every mile of lake, there are 10 miles of corrugated, wild ins-and-outs of

SOUTHEASTERN UTAH 119

A visit to Lake Powell is a real treat. (Courtesy Utah Travel Council)

red-rock canyon walls surrounding you. Perhaps the lake's appeal for boaters is that even though the lake is crowded, a quick cruise up any of a hundred side canyons can provide solitude and quiet. If you're on the lake at dusk, you'll notice boaters heading up these canyons, ready to stake out a private campsite for the night.

There are three marinas open year-round here, one on each side of the lake and one at the north end. All offer boat rentals, lodging, groceries, fuel, and myriad marina and fishing facilities. **Bullfrog Marina** is a full-scale resort, with a lodge and restaurant. Call (801) 684-3000 for information and reservations. **Halls Crossing** has "housekeeping units"—three bedroom suites, complete with a kitchen; call (801) 684-7000. **Hite** is the smallest marina, accessible off State Route 95. Call (801) 684-2278. Both Bullfrog and Halls Crossing have National Park Service campgrounds. A fourth large marina, **Wahweap**, is on the south end of Lake Powell, across the border in Arizona. For more information call (502) 645–2433.

Every possible size and shape of watercraft is available for rent at Lake Powell. A popular choice is a houseboat—its size and speed lend themselves to floating in and out of the lake's canyons. This water is perfect for waterskiing, and speed boats are prolific here.

If you don't have access to a private watercraft, an outing on a guided boat is an enjoyable way to tour the lake. Several outfitters take tourists on a day-long trip to **Rainbow Bridge National Monument**. This is the largest stone bridge yet discovered, and is often cited as one of the seven natural wonders of the world. Ancient Navajos believed that Rainbow was a sacred place. The bridge spans 275 feet and rises 290 feet from its rocky base. Until the dam created Lake Powell, Rainbow Bridge was accessible only by a two-day hike over red rock. Now it is accessible only by water. Several hundred thousand people now dock at the small marina each year and take the short walk to the bridge. While you're standing under it, remember that the capitol building in Washington, D.C., could fit under the bridge with plenty of room to spare. Tours to Rainbow Bridge leave from both Bullfrog and Halls Crossing in the morning and return in mid-afternoon. Travelers have a choice of sitting on an upper-deck level in the wind, or down below where it's easier to hear the guide describe the surrounding scenery and its history. The boat docks at Rainbow Bridge for about an hour. The cost is $72.00 for adults and $39.80 for children eleven and under and includes a box lunch and drinks. Call (801) 684-2261 for more information.

Another fun way to see Lake Powell, and that doesn't require an entire day, is to cross with the **John Atlantic Burr Ferry**. This hulking steel machine seems to defy the laws of flotation, as its 245 tons displace 100 tons of water. Eight cars and two buses fit on board, and the cost is about $9.00 per passenger vehicle. The ferry crosses from Bullfrog to Halls Crossing and back, on the hour, seven days a week, for most of the year. It always begins at 8:00 A.M., however quitting time depends on the season. The crossing takes about twenty minutes. There's an observation deck high above the water that offers great views. John Atlantic Burr was a pioneer rancher born to an immigrant mother while crossing the Atlantic Ocean. For ferry information call (801) 684–7000.

For more information on Lake Powell and Glen Canyon National Recreation Area, write P.O. Box 1507, Page, AZ, 86040, or call (520) 645–2471.

MEXICAN HAT

This is splendid, wide-open country; the Wild West made famous in cowboy movies and car commercials. It's also an area of the world where travelers are advised to keep plenty of water and snacks in their car, and a full tank of gas; services are few and far between. Just north of this town, look for two natural formations: The first is the unmistakable, sombreroed Spaniard for whom the town is named; the second is less distinct—a 15-mile-long strata of rock known as the **Navajo Rug**. **Valle's Trading Post** on the town's Main Street, Highway 163, sells cold drinks, good jewelry, and guide books.

For a great day-long adventure, head north from Mexican Hat on U.S. Highway 163, and watch for the intersection of State Road 261. Turn right and be ready to veer left for a trip to **Goosenecks of the San Juan State Park**, one of the better panoramas in the world. You'll look down a thousand feet, onto the tortured path of the San Juan River as it does an exaggerated series of S-curves, or goosenecks, through the Pennsylvania Hermosa Rock Formation. The river travels 6 miles, yet manages only a 1½ miles by the crow. Bathrooms are available, but don't look for a flush toilet. Call (801) 678–2238 for more information.

From the Goosenecks Road, get back on State Road 261, heading north, and hold on to your hat. You'll ascend the thousand-foot cliff wall of **Cedar Mesa**, heading nowhere but straight up. The steep switchbacks you encounter are called the **Moki Dugway**, named after an old mispronunciation of the word "Hopi." This road is an aerial thrill—be sure and stop near the top at the **Muley Point Overlook**. You're standing a thousand feet above Valley of the Gods, which in turn, rises a thousand feet above the San Juan River. This road was blasted up the side of this mountain during the uranium boom forty years ago. Since then it has been improved numerous times and today is fully paved and does not require a four-wheel-drive vehicle. Traveling on it does, however, require some old-fashioned intestinal fortitude.

Once you've reached the top of the mesa and have collected yourself, it's onward on State Road 261. You'll pass **Grand Gulch** on your left, a treasured area for backpackers. The Anasazi Indians flourished here 2,000 years ago, and many of their ruins and rock-art panels can be seen for those willing to make a long trek. There are no roads suitable for automobiles in the Gulch, but if your family can withstand the rigors of backpacking, this is a wonderful place to discover beauty and solitude. For more information call the Bureau of Land Management at (801) 587–2141.

Past Grand Gulch, it is just a few more miles to **Natural Bridges National Monument**. This place celebrates three natural stone bridges that have formed in the Cedar Mesa sandstone. The bridges are seen from viewpoints along a 9-mile, paved loop road, or by walking a trail that takes you close-up to the bridges.

Now, just because these bridges look similar to the stone arches you have seen elsewhere, don't be thinking they are the same thing. These massive stone spans began to be formed when dinosaurs roamed the earth. When harder stone was sedimented over softer stone, and the softer stone eroded out, these bridges are what remained. Natural Bridges is open year-round. The entrance fee of $4.00 is good for seven days. There is a 13-site campground, but there are no services here, and water is available only at the visitor center. Camping is $5.00 per night. You might notice the solar panels that supply all the electricity here. This monument was chosen as a test base for the use of solar energy in the mid-1980s. When it was built, this system was the largest sun-powered plant in the world.

TOP ANNUAL EVENTS FOR THE FAMILY IN SOUTHEASTERN UTAH

Music Festival, September, Moab, (801) 259-8825
White Mesa Ute Council Bear Dance, September, Bluff, (801) 587-3235
Parade of Lights, November, Bullfrog, (801) 684-3000
Fat Tire Festival, October, Moab, (801) 375-3231
Winter Festival, December, Moab, (801) 259-8825

If you're up for a challenge, the access trail to **Sipapu Bridge** is a lot of fun. It involves a 600-foot descent on wooden ladders and steel stairs and is a great leg-stretch for kids who've been trapped in the car for several hours. The second bridge on the route, **Kachina Bridge**, is the most massive of the three. It is named for the prehistoric drawings on its abutment, which resemble kachina dolls. **Owachomo Bridge** is the last stop on the loop road; it's the smallest and most "fragile of the bridges," at 106 feet high and 9 feet thick. For information on camping, hiking, and sightseeing here, write Natural Bridges National Monument, P.O. Box 1, Lake Powell, 84533-0101, or call (801) 692-1234.

MONUMENT VALLEY

To reach this far corner of Utah, head southwest on Highway 163, and travel almost all the way to the Arizona border. All of the land you see, once you leave Mexican Hat, is Navajo tribal land.

From far away you'll notice the achingly beautiful, monolithic rock formations of **Monument Valley**, and once you've arrived you'll find a bustling, touristy visitor center, with several gift shops. There are fabulous views in every direction. Find the **mittens** – (hint: this is two monuments), **elephant, camel, three sisters, eagle,** and dozens more. If you want to get closer to "what's out there" you must hire a guide. You'll most likely be approached in the parking lot by someone who is willing to take you through the valley; if you prefer a more formal arrangement, ask inside.

Just down the road is **Goulding's Trading Post**, established in 1923 by the Goulding Brothers and now listed on the National Register of Historic Places. For many years this was the primary trading post for Navajo Indians. A museum at Goulding's re-creates the old trading post, provides a history of movies made in the area, and includes a room dedicated to the Navajo Nation. The museum is open daily from 8:00 A.M. to 9:00 P.M. and there is no admission fee. There is a sixty-two-room motel here, a nice gift shop, and a restaurant. A film describing the history of the valley can be seen for a small fee. Call (801) 727–3231. For more information on Monument Valley, write Monument Valley Navajo Tribal Park, Box 360289, Monument Valley, 84536, or call (801) 727–3353.

FOUR CORNERS

For those in your family who just have to experience everything, there is **The Four Corners**. From Bluff, take Highway 163 east through Navajo Country to Aneth, and keep on heading south. After a while you'll cross the Colorado border and see the signs for the Four Corners monument. It is a big slab of concrete, with two dissected lines painted in its center. During the tourist season, there are usually Navajo craft booths set up around the perimeter of the square. Put a hand and foot in each square, and then . . . you will be touching four states at once! The Four Corners is the only place anywhere where four states meet. You cannot get any farther southeast in Utah, no matter how hard you try.

If you decide to continue on from here, there are many good choices nearby in the three surrounding states. **Canyon de Chelly National Monument** in Arizona, **Chaco Culture National Historic Park** in New Mexico, and **Mesa Verde National Park** in Colorado are just a few of the outstanding adventures in this part of the world.

Southwestern Utah

This area of the state likes to promote itself as "Color Country," and it's easy to see why. On this tour of the southwest corner of Utah you will pass up, over, around, and through fir- and aspen-covered mountains, crystal blue lakes, flowered meadows, and some very respectable red rock.

Zion, Utah's oldest and most popular national park, is here, along with ethereal Bryce Canyon and a host of other nationally designated scenic spots. Enjoy world-class theater, catch a few rodeos, marvel at lots of wildlife, and manage to pack in a few unique shopping experiences.

This chapter moves geographically in a roundabout way, beginning and ending near Cedar City, with a notable, large leap in space from Boulder town to the city of Kanab. This progression does not always make sense for the traveler, and care should be taken to consult a map before planning a road trip.

CEDAR CITY

During the months of June through September, Cedar City transforms itself into an Elizabethan English village, and the entire town celebrates a world-class **Shakespeare Festival**. For more than thirty-five years the "Festival City" has treated audiences to an array of activities that encompass the "Shakesperience." The festival now includes four Shakespeare plays each summer as well as two other popular plays, all of which are performed on a rotating basis in the outdoor **Adams Shakespearean Theatre** and the

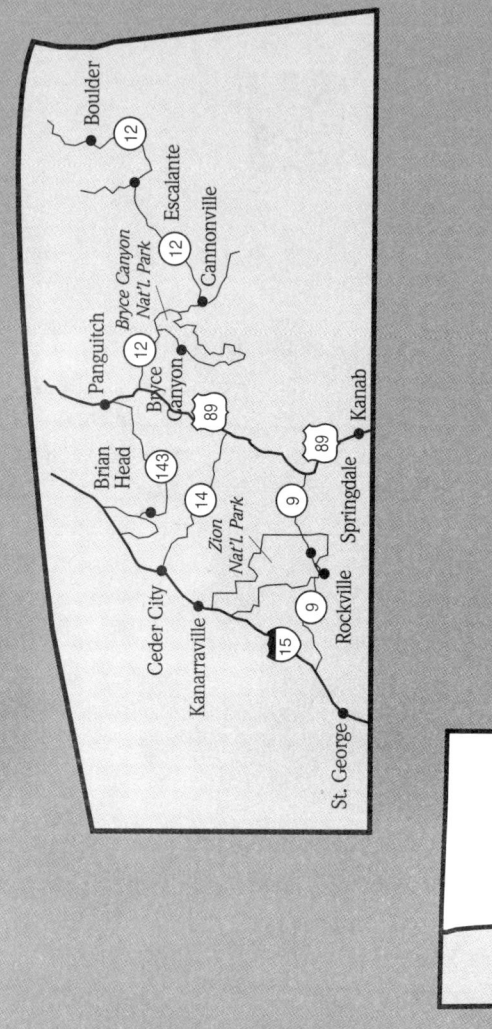

Southwestern Utah

Randall L. Jones Theatre. Tickets range from $10.00 to $35.00, and can be ordered by calling 800–PLAYTIX. Each evening at 7:30, before the performances, a **Greenshow** is played out on the grounds surrounding the theaters. Your children will love this free outdoor entertainment, which is billed as an "immersion into the song and dance of merrie olde England." On a typical night stages are set up on a huge, rolling lawn. Costumed performers may entertain by singing and dancing on one stage and performing farcical combat on the other. Puppeteers roam the grounds, as well as sellers of food, drink, and souvenirs. Another popular pre-play activity is **The Royal Feaste**, which takes place in Cedar City's junior high school, located right across the street from the Shakespeare Theater. The gym is altered to resemble the medieval world, and while dinner is served an amusing play takes place that involves much audience interaction. Your family will be served about seven courses, and eating with your fingers is encouraged. You will leave well versed in the Elizabethan mode of speech, and ready to tackle the Bard's flowery verse. The Royal Feaste is held Tuesday through Saturday and begins at 5:30 P.M. Tickets are $29.00, and must be reserved by noon the day of the Feaste. Call (801) 586–7878 for more information. Other fun things to do with a Shakespeare theme include a backstage tour, a field falconry, tour and week-long Shakespeare summer camps. Call (801) 586–7878 for information on prices, dates, and specifics of all Shakespeare Festival events.

A fun museum in town has unusual displays of old wagons, a cabin, and an Indian artifact collection donated by a man who lived with and was adopted by the Paiute Tribe. **Iron Mission State Park** also interprets the story of the development of the iron industry in the area. The museum is located at 585 North Main. Call (801) 586–9290 for more information.

When you are in town, take an afternoon to visit **Cedar Breaks National Monument,** located about 20 miles from Cedar City. Follow Highway 14 to its junction with Highway 148, and then turn north to the monument. In a country filled with surprises, Cedar Breaks is one of the best surprises of all. This is a huge earthen coliseum, more than 2,000 feet deep and 3 miles across. It is surrounded by juniper and filled with spectacular colored rock and rock formations that have been shaped by millions of years of wind, rain, and snow. A 5-mile scenic drive around the perimeter

Ceader City's annual Shakespeare Festival takes everyone back in time.
(Courtesy Utah Travel Council)

features four lookouts that offer different perspectives on the view below. A great hiking trail for children is the 2-mile **Alpine Pond Trail,** which leads past intricate rock shapes, forest glades, and ponds. A thirty-site campground is open June through September, and has running water, rest rooms, and an amphitheater with nightly ranger talks. There is a $9.00 nightly free for camping. Cedar Breaks is generally closed in the winter due to snow. For more information on fees and special activities, call (801) 586–9451.

BRIAN HEAD

Just a five-minute drive from Cedar Breaks, this place has the distinction of being the highest town in Utah. It exists mostly as a resort, and its beautiful surroundings are an anomaly of aspen and fir in a red-rock world. Brian Head perches on top of a 10,000-foot-high plateau— the altitude makes for a super ski resort in winter and a cool oasis in summer. Biking is very popular here, and in warm weather the winter chair lift is outfitted with bike racks to transport cyclists and their gear up to **Mountain Bike Park**, which accesses 40 miles of single-track trails. The trails are marked like ski runs, so cyclists can choose their skill level before starting out. Guided horseback rides are also popular in these mountains. Brian Head boasts restaurants, shops, more than 1,500 lodging rooms, and special events all through the summer. In September the town hosts an **Oktoberfest** celebration, complete with German food, oom-pah bands, and a guided bike tour known as the **Fall Colors Fat Tire Ride.** For all event and lodging information in Brian Head, call (801) 677–2810.

PANGUITCH

This lovely town is architecturally significant for its old, red-brick homes. A hundred years ago the town operated a brick kiln; each man who worked there was given enough bricks to build his own house. Many of these structures remain and are still inhabited.

The **Paunsagaunt Wildlife Museum**, at 250 East Center Street, features a large collection of stuffed animals that are displayed in re-created outdoor scenes, acting as they might have when they were alive. You'll see a skunk climbing a tree, a cougar tracking game, a deer enjoying a sunny afternoon, and more. There is also a display of exotic game from Africa, India, and Europe. Collections of fossils, weapons, tools, and artifacts can also be seen. The museum is open every day from May 1 to November 1 from 9:00 A.M. to 10:00 P.M. Call (801) 676–2500 for more information.

By the by, *panguitch* is a Paiute Indian word for "big fish," which people are still catching today at nearby **Panguitch Lake**. For information on events and lodging in the area, call (800) 444–6689.

BRYCE CANYON AND VICINITY

Highway 12, which turns east from Highway 89 just a few miles south of Panguitch, is a stunning drive and a destination unto itself. Your children will ooh and ahh as you pass through Dixie National Forest's **Red Canyon**, and experience the thrill of driving beneath two rock "tunnels." The Visitor Center at Red Canyon has good information about how and why this small patch of land, in the middle of a forest, is blessed with some of the brightest red rock anywhere. Guided horseback rides are available, and if you ask you will most likely be taken back into the untouched areas of the canyons to see a favorite hideout of outlaw Butch Cassidy. The campground here is very pleasant, and sites are available on a first come, first served basis. For camping information, call the Forest Service office in Panguitch at (801) 676-8815.

Bryce Canyon National Park is 8 miles east of Red Canyon, but just before you reach the park entrance, you'll come across a destination resort known as **Ruby's Inn**. The history of this place actually pre-dates the park, and its owners had much to do with the park's inception. The third generation of Ruby Syrett's family now runs the resort, which is a year-round amalgam of things to do. Besides the usual lodging, swimming, grocery, camping, and restaurant services, Ruby's contracts for open-cockpit biplane rides over the park, helicopter and other charter flights, as well as van tours and park shuttles. Guided horseback and buggy rides to the canyon rim are available in the warm-weather months, and chuckwagon dinners complete with Western hoedowns can be booked Memorial Day through September. Your children will especially enjoy the Petting Farm at Ruby's, where various barnyard pets can be fed, as well as the nightly rodeo that shows off the considerable horse sophistry of the families and children who live in the area. In winter cross-country skiing is popular on miles of groomed trails. For reservations and seasonal information about Ruby's Inn, call (801) 834-5341.

At long last, you will reach the reason for the city of hotels you have just passed—**Bryce Canyon National Park**. You will not be disappointed. Bryce is the "fairy princess" of Utah's national parks, and its hundreds of acres of densely placed, delicate pink spires and turrets are the most feminine of rock formations anywhere. The early Anglo settlers' names for the rocks remain today—Queen's Garden, the Grand Staircase, and Fairy Castle, to name a few. Earlier Paiute Indian residents saw the rocks in a more surreal light. They named the area Land of the Legend People, and believed the chimney-shaped rocks were evil folks who had been turned to stone, right in the midst of saying bad things. If you're ever down inside the canyon at dusk, look up at the monolith "faces," and remember this legend—you'll know just what those Indians had in mind. The park takes its name from one of the first Mormon pioneers who tried to run cattle in the area. Ebenezer Bryce will forever be remembered by his statement of exasperation over the myriad hiding places in the canyon: "It's a hell of a place to lose a cow!"

Bryce is not really a canyon at all, but a high plateau with hundreds of amphitheaters carved from its southern effacement. Water is the principal architect here, with sudden summer storms sending rushing water from the top of the plateau down into the soft sandstone and winter ice and snow helping the erosive process with their freeze-thaw cycle. The spires that remain are topped by harder, protective rock called capstone, which helps stave off the water's effects.

The top of the plateau remains intact, and is a surprise to people who come looking for the rock expanses and sunset colors for which Bryce is famous. The flat top of Bryce supports a vast evergreen forest and many kinds of wildlife. Wildflowers bloom throughout summer, spring, and fall. Autumn is a wonderful time to visit, when the aspens turn bright yellow against the green of the pines. One note of warning: The ground squirrels in the area have become so tame that they harbor no fear of humans. Don't feed these animals—park signs everywhere warn that they may carry disease.

Bryce is easily navigated. The 20-mile-long, two-lane road that follows the rim of the canyon neatly widens at each of twelve major viewpoints. At Bryce you don't have to work to see the big views—they're staring at you right there through your windshield, or even better, just a few steps out of your car to the plateau's very edge.

Fairyland Point is located just inside the park boundary, and you'll see its turn-off sign before you reach the pay station. You're overlooking Fairyland Canyon here, a petite, self-contained bowl well worth the mile drive off the main road. Immediately after passing the pay station, you'll find the Visitor Center on your left. This is a good place for all sorts of information including weather, hikes, wildflowers, ranger talks, and an orientation slide show. If you would like to take a guided walk with a ranger, ask for the schedule. You will also find rest rooms here.

Next up are **Sunrise** and **Sunset Points**, with their exponentially expanded views. You're overlooking the Bryce Amphitheater from both of these pull-outs, and it seems as if you can see most of the world in the distance. Closer up, just below the concrete, find the famous exposed-root pine trees, which continue in a most steadfast way to survive, even though their underpinnings are continually being washed downward. Notice the birds that enjoy showing off their skills here, swooping through the canyon and making sudden, picture-perfect stops on top of the pinnacles.

Inspiration Point is a favorite viewpoint because of its vista of **Silent City**. If you've seen any of a dozen science fiction movies that portray an abandoned metropolis, you'll have something of an idea of Silent City's power. Narrow ridges topped by thousands of delicate spindles lie packed together, resembling the most ethereal, golden-pink interpretation of urbanity. It's made absolutely eerie by its lack of emanating sound—in other words, this is well worth the short climb down a trail to get a better look.

Following a spur road from Inspiration, you'll reach **Paria Viewpoint,** where you'll look down 500 feet and beyond, witnessing the work of the Paria River. The cliffs that span out from this point are "failing," in geographical terms. Their broken spines have quit trying to shake off the prevailing erosional forces, and are quietly, magnificently, being returned to the canyon floor. Luckily for your family, this process will take another thousand or so years, and your children's children will look out on approximately this same view. Nearby is **Bryce Point,** also named after Ebenezer Bryce. Mr. Bryce built a road from his canyon-floor ranch to the bottom of these cliffs, for the purpose of transporting wood. Folks took to calling the area "Bryce's Canyon," and the name stuck.

Farview Viewpoint is aptly, though not exactly inspirationally, named. Look for **Molly's Nipple,** a most interesting formation for the grade-schoolers in your family, and look more closely for the big natural bridge down below.

Natural Bridge, Agua Canyon, Ponderosa Canyon, and **Yovimpa Point** follow, in full splendor.

And then the last stop, **Rainbow Point**. Here is a world-class view, and also a world-famous pine tree. The pine is a bristlecone, and when you look at this old, gnarled thing you may wonder why it's noteworthy. It is because this tree and its relatives are thought to be the longest living things on the planet. This particular specimen is about 1,800 years old, and it has survived by being tough and frugal with its resources. During drought years these pines actually kill off parts of themselves in order to save other parts. During years of heavy rainfall they soak up moisture and keep it in their secret places. The needles on the tree remain for decades.

The turn-off viewpoints are wonderful, but to really get the feel of Bryce, take a hike down into the canyon and surround yourself with rock formations. Three are about twenty-three self-guided walking trails in the park, and more than a dozen are well-managed by children. Bring water and snacks along in a day pack, and take it easy. Bryce's elevation is about 8,000 feet, and the thin air can leave you breathless. One more word of caution: The trails are carved from the surrounding rock, and they often are sprinkled by tiny stones that can act as ball bearings for human feet. The drop-offs from many of the trails are sheer cliffs, so be careful.

If you don't have all day, two good hikes to choose are **Navajo Loop** and **Queen's Garden Trail**. Navajo Loop trailheads at Sunset Point, and travels 1¼ miles past some of Bryce's more famous landmarks. You've probably seen pictures of **Thor's Hammer** (next to Delicate Arch in Arches National Park, perhaps the most photographed piece of stone in Utah), and if so, you'll recognize it on this trail. Look for **The Pope**, **Two Bridges**, and the wedded pine trees that, together, have managed to find their place in the sun. Near its end (or beginning, depending on which direction you choose), this trail takes you up a steep set of switchbacks. A short side trail leads to a view of Silent City, which is described above. Queen's Garden Trail is 1½ miles or so, down and back up the canyon, courtesy of a self-guided, signpost-marked tour. This trail begins at Sunrise Point and ends at Queen's Garden, named after the big stone face of Queen Victoria that peers from on high. There are rest benches here, which you may want to use before you turn around and head back out and up this nonloop trail.

If you do have all day and your children are feeling adventurous, you might want to try the **Rim Trail,** which travels 11 miles (yes, 11, but the trail is fairly level and this hike is rated easy-to-moderate) from Fairyland Point to Bryce Point. Take a lot of food and water and prepare for much picture taking on this most-scenic hike. If you get tired along the way, you can always veer off at any of the carpark view points, and figure out a way to get back to your own automobile.

> **MARGARET'S TOP FAMILY ADVENTURES IN SOUTHWESTERN UTAH**
>
> 1. Hiking the Queen's Garden Trail in Bryce Canyon National Park
> 2. Hiking to Emerald Pools in Zion National Park
> 3. Coral Pink Sand Dunes
> 4. Calf Creek Falls
> 5. Anasazi Indian Village State Park

Another suggestion is tackling a section of the **Under-the-Rim Trail**, which travels the entire length of the canyon for 22.5 miles, between Bryce Point and Rainbow Point. Consider coming back for another visit and backpacking the entire rim trail, which takes two to three days to complete and requires a heavy backpack and a lot of steep up-and-downs. Information on permits, water, and campsites is found at the Visitors Center.

A good rule of thumb is to hike the park early in the morning. One reason is that Bryce is a south-facing canyon and the morning light is spectacular. If you have the wherewithal to get to Sunrise Point at sunrise, clouds permitting, you'll have an unforgettable experience. Another reason for early morning hikes is the heat and crowds at Bryce in the summer months. (Bryce's high elevation makes for snowy and cold winters and fewer visitors, so attendance is down.) A workable plan is to get up early, hike a few miles, then have breakfast at beautiful **Bryce Canyon Lodge**, which is located inside the park, and then take the loop drive and stop and ogle at every one of the pull-outs.

Another fun way to see the park is on horseback. **Canyon Trailrides** offers two-hour and half-day trips into the canyon, for fees of $26.50 and

$37.10 respectively. Children five and older are allowed on the shorter ride, ages eight and older are allowed on the longer ride. The sign-up counter for the rides is located inside the park lodge, however advance reservations are strongly recommended. Call (801) 679–8665 for more information.

Bryce is open year-round, and a trip here in winter features stunning views. Picture pink-rock spires, covered with a white dusting, against a surround of electric blue sky. It's not wise to try and explain the power of beauty to anyone, but if you're going to have an epiphany, Bryce Canyon in winter is a pretty good locale. Snowshoes are loaned from the Visitor Center on a first-come basis. It is great fun for older children to strap these old, luggy things on their feet and attempt a few miles down and up the winter trails. Cross-country skiing along the plateau's edge is also an excellent way to spend a day.

The park fee is $5.00 per car, and is good for seven days. There are a lodge and two campgrounds inside the park, along with a restaurant, grocery store, and gas station. North and Sunset campgrounds open in late spring and close when water starts to freeze in the fall. They have a total of 218 sites, available on a first-come basis. No reservations are accepted. An overnight fee of $8.00 is charged. There is one group campsite available. These sites are prized, and the campground is almost always full, so be prepared to make other lodging arrangements. Call (801) 834–5322 for campground information. The lodge is open April through October, and Western cabins and motel rooms are also available. Advance reservations are highly recommended, and can be made by calling (303) 297–2757. For all information, including campground, area lodging, and overnight facilities, call Bryce Canyon National Park at (801) 834–5322 or write P.O. Box 170001, Bryce Canyon, 84717.

CANNONVILLE

Just south of this small ranching town is one of the weirder configurations of rock formations you will ever see, and that's a promise. A unique geologic history has fashioned the rock here into free-standing petrified sand pipes and petrified geysers, which jut up all over a valley known as **Kodachrome Basin State Park.** The name reflects the colors of the rock, which glow surrealistically at sunrise and sunset, and change shades throughout the day. Several marked hiking trails weave throughout the basin, and offer a closer look at this natural oddity. Biking on these trails is another good way to see the park. Find the basin by traveling 9 miles south of Cannonville on a partially-paved road. The campground here has hot showers and rest rooms. A concessionaire provides horseback and stagecoach rides. For reservations and general information, call (801) 679–8562. A short side trip from the park leads to **Grosvenor Arch,** a huge double arch that is well worth the effort of finding it. This road is passable only in good weather.

ESCALANTE

The isolated area surrounding Escalante is one of the last frontiers to be explored in the United States. It was not mapped until the mid-1800s, and the Pony Express carried mail here through the first part of this century. Today Escalante offers all of the modern amenities—lodging, restaurants, gas, and a great park for kids. **Escalante State Park** is a vast storehouse of petrified wood—huge pieces; tiny, twisted pieces; and everything in between. The park's two trails wind past fallen forests that have turned to rock, the bones of ancient dinosaurs, and petroglyphs and remnants of ancient Indian dwellings. Amazingly, there is a wetland bird viewing site in the park—one of the few in southern Utah. **Wide Hollow Reservoir** rims the park, and trout fishing is popular here. Escalante State Park is found just west of town. It has a visitor center and campground. Advance reservations can be made by calling (800) 322–3770 during business hours. Day use and camping fees are charged. For more information on the park, call (801) 826-4466.

Twelve miles east of Escalante on Highway 12 is one of the better children's hikes in the state—the 2½-mile walk to **Calf Creek Falls**. The falls are located inside the **Calf Creek National Recreation Area,** and the turn-off sign is well marked along the roadside. Don't be put off by the 5-mile total length of this walk—grab a brochure and head out. There are about twenty-two marked points of interest on this fairly level trail, including views of spectacular petroglyphs and Anasazi ruins, pioneer farming artifacts, and numerous wildlife. If you get tired, it's easy to turn around. But if your children make it to the canyon terminus, they will be rewarded with a spectacular waterfall that plunges from atop a sandstone cliff. On a hot day this is a perfect place to take off your shoes and wade in the cold water. If you have the luck to find yourselves alone at the falls, this is also a nice place for a picnic. Back at the trailhead is a campground with rest rooms and water. Campsites are available on a first-come basis for $7.50 per night. For more information on Calf Creek, call (801) 826-4291.

Back out on Highway 12, keep heading east for one of the most thrilling car rides anywhere. When you approach **Hell's Backbone**, you'll know it. This twisty section of the road falls away dramatically on either side, leaving no room for error on the part of the driver. What you see spread out below is called **Box Death Hollow**, and it is a favorite primitive area for backpackers.

BOULDER

Just getting to this town is an adventure. To the north the road leads through the **Dixie National Forest**, with myriad hiking and camping possibilities. To the south is some of the most dramatic desert country in the world. Due east is the **Burr Trail**, a partly-paved road that twists and careens all the way to Lake Powell. Smack in the midst of it all is little Boulder, for years a quiet ranching community, and just now beginning to take on the look of a tourist destination.

A park in town pays tribute to the area's ancient inhabitants. **Anasazi Indian Village State Park** preserves the site of one of the largest Anasazi communities west of the Colorado River, occupied by "the ancients" from 1050 to 1200 A.D. The visitor center here does an excellent job of interpreting ancient life, and just beyond it are real artifacts and ruins that are accessed on self-guided trails. For park information, call (801) 335-7308.

KANAB

Countless Western movies have been filmed in and around this "authentic" looking town, and sometimes Kanab is known as "Little Hollywood." Several of the movie sets remain as tourist attractions. **Old Paria** was built in 1963 for the movie *Sergeants Three* and it still stands, just a few miles off Highway 89 between Kanab and Lake Powell. Nine miles from Kanab on Highway 89 is the **Johnson Canyon** set, where all of the outdoor scenes from the TV series *Gunsmoke* were filmed. It is open for tours during the summer and visitors may walk down the streets and peer inside the vacant buildings of Dodge.

Picture fine sand the color of the inside of an exotic sea shell. Then picture tall hills of this sand stretching for as far as your eyes can see. You will now have an idea of what **Coral Pink Sand Dunes State Park** looks like. This mind-blowing place is just 12 miles west of Highway 89, but several planets from Earth in terms of scenery. For several thousand years the surrounding colorful rock has been evolving into these dunes, and the result is a huge playground of bright pink sand. Needless to say, photographic opportunities are many. Children will enjoy hiking on the nature trail and the short boardwalk trail that leads to an overlook. Drivers of off-highway vehicles love this park, too. The park is open year-round, and has a campground with rest rooms and showers. There is an entrance fee to the park of $3.00 per car and camping is $11.00 per night. Call (801) 648–2800 for park information, and (800) 322–3770 for camping reservations.

SPRINGDALE

The big deal around these parts is **Zion National Park**. The park literally surrounds the town of Springdale, and if you're driving from the direction of Kanab, you'll pay a fee at the park's eastern entrance and drive Highway 9 through the park before reaching Springdale. Zion is a friendly, grand old national park, and one of the most family-oriented places in Utah. There are many small, fun hikes here, with stupendous scenery along the way and stunning scenic finales at trail's end. There are hundreds of flowers, animals, and rock formations to identify and make up names for, and even in the hottest summer weather there is always a shady picnic spot to be found in **Zion Canyon**.

If Zion seems tame and orderly compared to Utah's other national parks, it could be because of its longevity and history. Zion is Utah's first park, and one of the oldest national parks in the nation. A section of the current park was set aside as a monument in 1909 by President Taft. In 1918 the monument was enlarged and given the name Zion. In 1919 it was made a national park by an act of Congress. Many of Zion's trails and viewpoints were marked and interpreted decades ago. Most of the trails are hard-packed, and some are even paved. There's a feeling here that the area is comfortable and safe.

The park's size may also be a factor in its homey feeling. While the actual boundaries are immense—147,000 acres—Zion Canyon, where most tourists congregate and the aforementioned small hikes are located, is relatively small. About 6 miles long, the canyon is as deep as it is wide until it terminates at **The Narrows**, a seasonally-hikable section averaging 2,000-foot-high cliffs and a stream bed 50 feet wide. The canyon's 6 miles contain about 60,000 miles worth of scenery. Anyone who has wandered in Zion's sandstone glow, or ventured into its cool grotto canyons, knows that words are not enough to explain its appeal. Visitors young and old alike are awestruck by its magnigicent splendor. Famous natural stone landmarks such as **The Watchman, The Sentinel, Court of the Patriarchs,** and **Mountain of the Sun** must be viewed at least once in a lifetime. It is said that nonreligious explorers named many of the stone monuments here, but that none other than religious terms could be found to describe Zion's grandeur. You'll notice that temples, cathedrals, patriarchs, thrones, and angels are common. The **Virgin River,** original architect of the landscape, runs a green, glazy course through the red rock, and still continues its canyon design, carrying the equivalent of 180 carloads of ground rock out of the park each day.

Some of the hikes best suited for children are the trails to **Weeping Rock,** a half-mile, self-guided trail, ending at a rock alcove that features dripping springs and hanging gardens of wildflowers; **Emerald Pools,** a 1.2-mile round trip that leads past three waterfalls and the small pools they have created; and **Riverside Walk,** a paved 2-mile walk that follows the Virgin River upstream, past hanging gardens and marshy wetlands, to The Narrows. The trail to **Angels Landing** and the **West Rim** is a more challenging hike for young children, but it has sections along the way, such as **Walter's Wiggles** and **Refrigerator Canyon** (where early inhabitants once stored their perishables), that work as a hike terminus.

The **Canyon Overlook** hike requires a drive out of Zion Canyon along Mt. Carmel Highway to just east of a long tunnel. This 1-mile in-and-out trail passes under low-hanging rocks and by (but not too close to) steep drop-offs to end at a spectacular viewpoint of Zion and Pine Creek canyons. A good guidebook that interprets the plant and animal life along this trail is available at the Visitor Center. And speaking of **Zion's long tunnel,** you'll want to take a drive through this engineering marvel, constructed in 1930. It carves through rough terrain to connect lower Zion Canyon with the high plateaus to the east. Look around when you enter, because when you exit the landscape will look very different. On one side are the massive cliff walls of Zion Canyon, and on the other are fantastically eroded colorful sandstone formations. Be sure to notice **Checkerboard Mesa,** which is criss-crossed with cracks into a surprisingly geometric pattern.

Watching nature is a favorite pastime at Zion, and the park is very obliging with its diversity and depth of watchables. In spring, summer, and fall showy flowers can be seen. Look for the purple Zion daisy and the bright red cardinal monkeyflower, two of a family of 899 plant species found in the park. More than sixty species of birds are permanent residents, as well as sixty-eight species of mammals, thirty-six different reptiles and seven amphibians. To help children ages six through twelve learn about the natural environment, Zion offers a Junior Ranger Program, held during the summer at the Zion Nature Center.

The **Visitor Center** in the park is located at the south entrance, and is open daily all year from 9:00 A.M. to 4:30 P.M., with longer hours in the summer. The congenial rangers here will help you plan a visit that fits the needs of your family; you'll also find books, topographic maps, and free brochures. There are exhibits explaining the area and a descriptive film that is shown every half hour.

The two campgrounds in this section of the park are open on a first-come basis. Both have fire grates, picnic tables, water, and modern rest rooms. **Zion Lodge,** located inside Zion Canyon, features motel units and rustic cabins as well as a restaurant and gift shop. Advance reservations are recommended; call (303) 297–2757 for lodging information. Open-air tram tours of the park are a great way to get acquainted with the park's narrow, winding roads. Ask for a schedule at Zion Lodge. Guided horseback rides are available from May through October. Make reservations at the lodge, or by calling in advance: (801) 772–3801. A park entrance fee of $5.00 per car or $2.00 per walk-in is charged, and there is a camping fee

TOP ANNUAL EVENTS FOR THE FAMILY IN SOUTHWESTERN UTAH

Arts Festival, Easter weekend, St. George, (801) 634-5850
Junior Ranger program, summer, Zion National Park, (801) 772-3256
Rodeo, May through September, Ruby's Inn, (801) 834-5341
Shakespeare Festival, June through September, Cedar City, (801) 586-7878
Oktoberfest, September, Brian Head, (801) 677-2810

of $8.00 per night. For more information on the good fun that awaits you at Zion National Park, call (801) 772-3256, or write Springdale, 84767.

When you've finished with Zion's natural wonders, head back into Springdale for a man-made adventure at the local **Zion Canyon Cinemax Theater**. The film shown here was made especially for Zion, and is known as *Treasure of the Gods*. It is thirty-seven minutes long, shown on the hour, and is designed "to enhance the visitor's Zion National Park experience by exploring Zion's hidden treasures and legends." The 500-seat theater is famous for having one of the world's largest screens (six stories high by 80 feet wide), and its effect is to draw you inside the action and make you feel one with the film. The theater complex is found at 145 Zion Park Boulevard, and includes a visitor center, gift shop, book store, art gallery, deli, and picnic areas. Admission to the theater is $7.00 for adults and $4.50 for children. Call (801) 772-2400 for more information.

Another summer night's outing can be enjoyed outdoors at the **O. C. Tanner Amphitheater**. There, a rousing multimedia production called *The Grand Circle; A National Park Odyssey* spotlights the eight national parks and other scenic wonders that are within a day's drive of Springdale.

The program is projected onto a large screen, with the cliffs of Zion acting as a dramatic backdrop. Tickets are $4.00 for adults, $3.00 for children, or $10.00 per family. For more information, call (801) 652–7994.

ROCKVILLE

There are several lovely bed and breakfasts in this tiny berg that cater to visitors to Zion National Park. But if you cross the river and head about 2 miles west of Rockville, you will see the signed turn-off for **Grafton,** one of the better preserved ghost towns in the West. Grafton was originally settled by Mormon farmers in the 1860s, but disease, floods, and a war with the Blackhawk Indians caused the town to be abandoned early in the twentieth century. Several buildings here are still fairly intact—a brick church is the most notable. If you and your children have seen the movie *Butch Cassidy and the Sundance Kid*, you might recognize Grafton as the backdrop of the bicycle scene. A short distance north of town is its old cemetery, where the grave markers make an interesting historic record.

ST. GEORGE

Just a decade or so ago St. George was a sleepy desert town, known mostly as a gas stop on the way to Las Vegas. Much has changed since then. Because of its favorable climate, St. George's population has grown exponentially in the last ten years. Its main street is now a mile-long shopping, eating, and lodging opportunity. But there is one constant in St. George, and that is the beauty of its surrounding landscape. Wonderful hikes and biking trails for children, as well as beautiful canyons and vistas, rim the town.

The city's mild winter climate was not lost on the early pioneers. During Brigham Young's lifetime, St. George was winter headquarters for the Mormon Church, especially during the last years of his life when he suffered from rheumatism, Young spent much time here. His century-old **winter home** and the surrounding grounds have been restored and can be toured daily from 9:00 A.M. to dusk. There is no admission fee. The house is located at 67 West 200 North. Another Mormon who figured prominently in St. George's history is Jacob Hamblin. The **Jacob Hamblin home** has been restored and turned into a living museum. Hamblin is remembered for his work as a colonizer and peacemaker with local Native Americans. The house was built in 1862, and its construction and architecture reflect the primitive conditions of that time. Separate quarters for Hamblin's multiple wives and a variety of pioneer artifacts can be seen here. **St. George's Mormon Temple**, found at 440 South 300 East, is another interesting place to visit. The actual temple is open only to Mormon faithful, but the grounds are available to everyone. Volunteers in the visitor center will give tours and explain local history. When you are here, be sure to ask if you can visit the Contemplation Room, where a simulated desert storm works its magic in a dry landscape. The visitor center is open daily from 9:00 A.M. to 9:00 P.M. There is no admission charge. Call (801) 673–5181 for more information.

For a more raucous outing, head for **Fiesta Family Fun Center** at 171 East 1160 South. This huge entertainment complex has go carts, bumper boats, batting cages, mini golf, a video arcade and driving range, and of course pizza and snacks to appeal to every young appetite. All activities are paid for individually, although books of tickets may be purchased. Hours are 10:00 A.M. to 10:00 P.M. Monday through Thursday and 10:00 A.M. to 11:00 P.M. on Friday and Saturday. Call (801) 628–1818 for more information.

One of the state's better outlet-center malls is found on the eastern edge of town. **Zion Factory Stores**, located at St. George Boulevard's junction with Interstate 15, features high-end, name-brand merchandise at discount prices. The mall has food service and rest rooms and is open six days a week from 10:00 A.M. to 8:00 P.M. and Sunday from 10:00 A.M. to 5:00 P.M. For more information call (801) 674–9800.

St. George is a favorite destination for spring vacationers, because T-shirt weather arrives here much earlier than in the colder, northern part of the state. If you happen to be one of the flock of tourists who arrive here for Easter weekend, you'll want to check out the **Arts Festival**, held on Friday and Saturday, from 10:00 A.M. until dusk. Several blocks on Main Street are closed off to traffic for this event, which features hundreds of fine art booths, as well as food and entertainment. A special area is set aside for children, with games, crafts, and scheduled performances especially geared for a younger age group. Call (801) 634–5850 for more information.

One of the canyons near town is so spectacular it has been preserved as a state park. **Snow Canyon State Park** is a relatively small area with a vast collection of geologic wonders. Volcanic cones, deep red sandstone cliffs, twisted layers of rock, and sand dunes populate the narrow area between two steep cliff walls. An official scenic backway charts a paved path through the canyon, and it is possible to see its beauty without leaving your car. But, of course, a better experience is gained by hiking or biking in the canyon, or taking advantage of the guided horse trips that are available here. A surprising array of plants and animals thrive in this desert climate, including three endangered species: the peregrine falcon, desert tortoise, and gila monster. Petroglyphs and ruins are evidence that the area was occupied by the Anasazi Indians more than 800 years ago. The park is open year-round, but summer can be uncomfortably hot. Try to time your visit during the months of October through May for optimum weather—which brings up the subject of snow: Snow Canyon rarely receives any. It is named after a pair of pioneer settlers by the name of Snow (their first names were Lorenzo and Erastus). Find Snow Canyon by following Highway 18 northwest from St. George for 10 miles. A thirty-six-unit campground with rest rooms and showers is open year-round, and reservations are accepted. Call (801) 628–2255 for park information.

Just a short drive south is a theater with a truly stunning set. **Tuacahn** and its adjacent **Heritage Arts Center** host *UTAH!,* an epic musical drama that tells the story of this area's early pioneers and explorers. The backdrop for this production is the natural surround of a red-rock canyon. *UTAH!* is famous for its complicated special effects, which include lightning bolts, raging floods, cascading waterfalls, and howling coyotes. The production runs June through early October of each year, Monday through Saturday nights. When you order your tickets, ask about the Western Dutch-oven dinner that can be included in the evening's activities. For ticket prices and other information, call (800) 746–9882.

HURRICANE

This thriving small town was supposedly named after a whirlwind, which snapped the top off a settler's buggy and caused him to exclaim, "Well, that was a hurricane!" These days Hurricane is world headquarters for a company called **Chums,** which is famous for the manufacture of an item called an eyeglass retainer. The retainers fit onto your glasses and around the back of your head, saving you from losing your spectacles. Chums also makes caps, T-shirts and other cotton clothing, and everything comes in kids' and adult sizes. Their outlet store is found at 120 South Main and is open Monday through Friday from 9:00 A.M. to 6:00 P.M., and Saturday 10:00 A.M. to 6:00 P.M. Call (801) 635-9831 for more information.

From the Chums store it is just a few minutes drive to a really fun fishing pond. The pond is privately owned and you must follow some complicated directions before you can dip in your reel, but if your children love to fish it is well worth the effort. First, go to St. George to the Hurst Ben Franklin store and find the sporting goods section. Then ask about the trout pond at **Zion View Ranch.** A reservation will be made for you, and you will be issued a pass, which you must have when you go to the ranch. Transport yourself back to the Chum's store with your pass in your hand. Find the pond by heading left at Chums and going up the hill for three miles. At mile marker 19 turn right on a dirt road. You'll pass by a whole bunch of ostriches, which are the primary product of the ranch, and finally reach the pond. You can catch and release all the fish you want, or pay $4.00 a pound for the ones you want to keep. A pass is $40.00 per adult and $20.00 per child for a full day, and $30.00 per adult and $15.00 per child for a half-day of fishing. For more information, call (801) 673-6141.

KANARRAVILLE

This town is near the northwestern section of Zion National Park known as the **Kolob Canyons.** Find the turn-off to Kolob at Exit 40 on Interstate 15. Here an ancient stream has carved spectacular canyons from the stone of Kolob Terrace. Pick up a road guide at the visitor center, and then choose between two paved roads to see this area. The Kolob Canyons Road will take you 5 miles and a millenium back in time through Finger Canyons and terminate at a wonderful viewpoint: the Kolob Terrace Road overlooks the colorful cliffs of North Creek. A visitor center at the canyon entrance has a bookstore and rangers who will help you decide which of several hikes will best suit the abilities of your family. For more information on Kolob, call (801) 772-3256.

General Index

A

Adams Shakespearean Theatre, 125
Adobe Rock, 50
All 'Round Ranch, 92
Alpine, 55
Alpine Loop, 58
Alpine Pond Trail, 128
Alpine Slide, 45
Alta Ski Resort, 43
America's Freedom Festival (Provo), 65
American Fork, 57
American Fork Canyon, 57
Ansazi Indian Village State Park, 137
Antelope Island State Park, 5
Antelope Island Buffalo Round-Up, 5
Anticline Overlook, 113
Aquanoodle Slide, 91
Arches National Park, 104
Art City Days (Springville), 67
Ashley National Forest, 95
Assembly Hall, 29

B

Barrick Mercur Mine Visitors Center, 52
Bean Life Science Museum, 63
Bear Dance (Fort Duchesne), 88
Bear Lake, 23
Bear Lake Convention and Visitors Bureau, 24
Bear Lake Overlook, 23
Bear Lake State Park, 23
Bear River Migratory Bird Refuge, 16
Beaver Creek Lodge, 23
Beaver Mountain Ski Area, 22
Beehive House, 31
Belly Dance Festival, 38
Belmont Hot Springs, 17
B. F. Larsen Gallery (Provo), 64

Big Cottonwood Canyon, 42
Black and White Days (Richmond), 25
Black Diamond Stampede Rodeo (Price), 71
Blanding, 114
Blanding Dinosaur Museum, 114
Bluff, 115
Bluffdale, 47
BLM Office in Price, 72, 73, 75
Blue Mountain Trading Post, 114
Bonneville Cisco run (Bear Lake), 24
Bonneville Salt Flats, 53
Boulder, 137
Bluebird Cafe, 19
Bountiful, 1
Bountiful-Davis Art Center, 3
Bountiful Recreation Center, 3
Bountiful Mormon Temple, 3
Box Elder County Chamber of Commerce, 15
Brian Head, 128
Bridal Veil Falls, 66
Bridger Beach, 5
Brigham City, 15
Brigham City Mormon Tabernacle, 16
Brigham Young University, 63
Brigham Young's Winter Home, 142
Brighton Ski Resort, 42
Broadbents Family Department Store, 61
Browning Firearms Museum, 9
Browning-Kimball Classic Car Museum, 9
Brown's Park, 97
Bryce Canyon Lodge, 134
Bryce Canyon National Park, 129, 130
Buckhorn Draw, 74
Bullfrog Marina, 120

GENERAL INDEX

Burn's Saddlery, 80
Butch Cassidy Water Slide, 101

C
Cabin of Josie Bassett Morris, 94
Calf Creek National Recreation Area, 136
Camp Floyd State Park, 61
Cannonville, 135
Canyon de Chelly National Monument, 124
Canyon Overlook Trail, 139
Canyon Rims Recreation Area, 113
Canyon Trailrides, 134
Canyon View Park, 68
Canyonlands National Park, 108
Capitol Gorge, 80
Capitol Reef National Park, 77
Capitol Reef Scenic Drive, 79
Capitol Theatre, 34
Carbon County Travel Bureau, 71
Carvers Cove Horseback Rides, 13
Cascade Springs, 58
Castle Dale, 73
Cathedral Valley, 80
Cave Spring Trail, 110
Cedar Breaks National Monument, 127
Cedar City, 125
Cedar Mesa Pottery, 114
Cedar Pony, 115
Centerville, 3
Chaco Culture National Historic Park, 124
Chase Home Museum of Folk Art, 38
Cherry Hill Campground, 4
Chieftain Museum (Santaquin), 84
Christmas Lights at Temple Square, 30
Christmas Village (Ogden), 10

Chums, 145
City and County Building, 35
Classic Skating and Waterslides, 63
Cleveland, 73
Cleveland Lloyd Dinosaur Quarry, 73
College of Eastern Utah Prehistoric Museum, 70
Collett Art Gallery, 10
Colorado River, 102, 103, 118
Colorado River Scenic Byway, 104
Confluence of the Green and Colorado Rivers, 110, 111
Copperton, 47
Coral Pink Sand Dunes State Park, 138
Corona Arch, 103
Council Hall, 36
Cove Fort, 81
Cow Canyon Trading Post, 116
Cow Country Rodeo (Manila), 96
Coyote Run, 103
Crossroads Plaza, 33
Cub Creek Trail, 93
Crystal Geyser, 76
Crystal Hot Springs Resort, 17

D
Dan O'Laurie Canyon Country Museum (Moab), 101
Daughters of Utah Pioneers Museum (Logan), 19
Daughters of Utah Pioneers Museum (Ogden), 8
Daughters of Utah Pioneers Museum (Springville), 67
Daughters of Utah Pioneers Museum (Tooele), 51
Daughters of Utah Pioneers Museum (Vernal), 90

GENERAL INDEX

Days of '47 Rodeo (Salt Lake City), 34
Dead Horse Point State Park, 112
Deer Creek Reservoir and State Park, 59
Deer Valley Resort, 46
Delicate Arch, 106
Delta Center, 34
Deseret Peak, 51
Deseret Wilderness Area, 51
Desert Star Playhouse, 42
Desert Voices Trail, 93
Devil's Garden, 108
Devil's Kitchen, 84
Dinah Bowl, 91
Dinosaur Days (Vernal), 91
Dinosaur Gardens, 90
Dinosaur National Monument, 93
Dinosaur Round-Up Rodeo (Vernal), 91
Dinosaur Visitor Center and Quarry, 93
Dinosaurland Information Office, 88
Donner-Reed Museum, 50
Drive Through the Ages, 95
Duchesne, 87
Dutch John, 94

E

Eagle Canyon Overlook, 75
Eagle Gate, 32
Earth Science Museum (Provo), 63
Eccles Dinosaur Park, 11
Eccles Railroad Center, 9
Eden, 13
Edge of the Cedars State Park, 114
Egyptian Theater (Park City), 44
Electric Light Parade (Helper), 70
Eli Anderson's Wagons, 17
Ellen Eccles Theater, 19
Emerald Pools Trail, 139
Emery County Pioneer Museum, 73
Enola Gay Monument, 54
Ephraim, 83
Escalante, 136
Escalante State Park, 136
Eureka, 84

F

Factory Stores at Park City, 44
Fairfield, 61
Fairyland Canyon, 131
Fall Colors Fat Tire Bike Ride (Brian Head), 129
Family History Library, 32
Family Search Center, 31
Farmington, 3
Farmington Bay Waterfowl Management Area, 4
Fat Tire Festival (Moab), 103
Festival of Lights (Manila), 96
Festival of Lights (Spanish Fork), 68
Festival of the American West (Logan), 21
Festival of the Old West (Tooele), 52
Fiesta Family Fun Center, 143
Flaming Gorge Dam, 96
Flaming Gorge Flying Service, 96
Flaming Gorge Lodge, 96
Flaming Gorge National Recreation Area, 94
Flaming Gorge Recreation Services, 96
Field House of Natural History State Park, 88
Fiery Furnace, 105, 107
Fillmore, 82
Fort Buenaventura State Park, 8
Fort Douglas Military Museum, 38
Fort Duchesne, 88

GENERAL INDEX

Four Corners, 124
Free Flying Bird Show, 38
Fremont Indian State Park, 80
Fruit Heights, 4
Fruita, 78
Fruitway, 14
Fun City USA Water Slide Park, 9

G

Gallivan Utah Center, 35
Garden City, 23
Gardner Historic Village, 48
Geyser Pass, 102
Goblin Valley State Park, 76
Golden Onion Days (Payson), 85
Golden Spike National Historic Site, 15
Goosenecks of the San Juan State Park, 121
Grafton, 142
Grand Gulch, 122
Grand Wash, 78
Grantsville, 50
Great Salt Lake, 48
Great Salt Lake Desert, 52
Great Salt Lake State Park, 49
Greek Festival Days (Price), 71
Green River, 75, 96, 103
Green River City, 75
Green River Campground, 93
Green River State Park, 75
Green River Visitors Center, 75, 76
Greenshow, 127
Grosvenor Arch, 136

H

Hale Center Theater, 40
Halls Crossing, 120
Hanksville, 76
Hansen Planetarium, 33
Hardware Ranch, 17
Hatch River Expeditions, 94
Hatch Trading Post, 117
Head Start Days (Bluff), 116
Heber, 58
Heber Valley Historic Railroad, 58
Hell's Backbone, 137
Helper, 69
Helper Centennial Parkway, 70
Helper Intermountain Theatre, 70
Heritage Community Theater, 14
Heritage Days (Spring City), 83
Hickman Trail, 78
High Country Tours, 66
Hill Aerospace Museum, 7
Historic Benson Grist Mill, 50
Hite Marina, 120
Hog Canyon, 94
Hogle Zoological Gardens, 40
Hole-in-the-Rock, 115
Hole 'N the Rock, 113
Homestead Resort, 59
Hondoo Rivers and Trails, 75
Honeyville, 17
Horseshoe Canyon, 112
House of Copper, 48
Hovenweep National Monument, 117
Huck Finn Day (Provo), 65
Huck's Museum and Trading Post, 114
Hummingbird Hill Trail Rides, 26
Huntsville, 13
Huntsville Trappist Monastery, 13
Hurrah Pass, 103
Hurricane, 144
Hutchings Museum of Natural History, 60
Hyrum, 17

GENERAL INDEX

Hyrum City Museum, 18
Hyrum State Park, 18
Hydrosauras Slide, 91

I
Indian Day Celebration (Bluff), 116
Indian Trail, 12
Inspiration Point, 132
International Folk Festival (Price), 71
International Peace Gardens, 40
Iron Mission State Park, 127
Island In The Sky, 111

J
Jacob Hamblin Home, 142
Jardine Juniper Trail, 21
Jens Nielson House, 116
Jensen, 92
Jensen Living Historical Farm, 20
John Atlantic Burr Ferry, 121
John Jarvie Historic Ranch, 97
John Wesley Powell Museum (Green River), 75
Jones Hole National Fish Hatchery, 98
Johnson Canyon Movie Set, 137
Joseph Smith Memorial Building, 30

K
Kanab, 137
Kanarraville, 145
Kearns Mansion, 35
Kennecott Utah Copper Bingham Canyon Mine, 47
Kennecott Visitors Center, 48
Kimball Art Center, 44
Kodachrome Basin State Park, 135
Kolob Canyons, 145

L
Ladies of the White House Doll Collection, 90
Lagoon Amusement Park, 3
Lagoon-A-Beach, 4
Lake Flaming Gorge, 94
Lake Point, 48
Lake Powell, 118
Landscape Arch, 108
LaSal Junction, 113
LaSal Mountains, 102
Layton, 5
Layton Heritage Museum, 5
Layton/Ott Planetarium, 10
Layton Surf and Swim, 5
LDS Church Office Building, 32
Lehi, 60
Lehi Roller Mills, 61
Lehi Round-Up Rodeo, 61
Liberty Park, 37
Limber Pine Nature Trail, 22
Lion House, 32
Little Cottonwood Canyon, 42
Little Hole, 96
Little Miner's Park, 45
Little Sahara Sand Dunes, 83
Logan, 18
Logan Canyon, 21
Logan Center Street, 19
Logan Chamber of Commerce and Information Center, 19
Looking Glass Rock, 113

M
Maddox Restaurant, 14
Manila, 94
Manti, 82
Marble Park, 15
Marc II, 101

GENERAL INDEX

Marmalade Hill, 37
Martin Harris Pageant (Clarkston), 25
The Maze, 109
McCurdy Doll Museum, 64
MD Ranchhouse, 114
Melon Days (Green River), 76
Mesa Verde National Park, 124
Memory Grove, 36
Mercur, 52
Mesa Arch Trail, 111
Mexican Hat, 121
Midway, 59
Midway Aviation (Moab), 113
Miles Goodyear Cabin, 8
Millcreek Canyon (Moab), 103
Mills Junction, 50
Minnetonka Cave, 25
Moab, 99
Moab Information Center, 101
Moki Dugway, 122
Mom's Cafe (Salina), 80
Monticello, 114
Monticello Museum, 114
Monument Valley, 123
Mountain Man Rendezvous (Bear Lake), 23
Mormon Miracle Pageant, 82
Mormon Tabernacle Choir, 30
Mountain Bike Park, 129
Movie locations (Moab), 104
Muley Point Overlook, 122
Murray, 41
Museum of Art (Provo), 64
Museum of Church History and Art (Salt Lake City), 33
Museum of Peoples and Cultures (Provo), 63
Museum of the San Rafael, 74
Myra Powell Art Gallery, 9

N

Natural Bridges National Monument, 122
Navajo Loop Trail, 133
Navtech Expeditions, 102
Nebo Loop, 84
The Needles, 109
Needles Overlook, 113
Needles Visitor Center, 109
Nephi, 83
Newspaper Rock, 109
Nine Mile Canyon, 72
Nora Eccles Harrison Museum of Art, 20
Nordic Valley Ski Resort, 13
North American River Tours, 102

O

O.C. Tanner Amphitheater, 141
Ogden, 7
Ogden Bay Waterfowl Management Area, 12
Ogden Canyon, 12
Ogden Christmas Village, 10
Ogden Convention and Visitors Bureau, 14
Ogden's Historic 25th Street, 9
Ogden-Hof Winter Carnival, 11
Ogden Ice Sheet, 9
Ogden MormonTemple, 8
Ogden Natural History Museum (Union Station), 9
Ogden Natural History Museum (Weber State campus), 10
Ogden Nature Center, 11
Ogden River Parkway, 12
Ogden River Parkway Festival, 12
Oktoberfest (Brian Head), 129
Oktoberfest Snowbird), 43

GENERAL INDEX

Old Deseret Village, 39
Old Paria, 137
Oowah Lake, 102
Ophir, 52
Orem, 62
Oscar Swett Historic Ranch, 96
Outlaw Trail Festival (Vernal), 91

P
Pages Lane Theater, 3
Panguitch, 129
Panguitch Lake, 129
Paradise Pone, 57
Park City, 43
Park City Arts Festival, 44
Park City Chamber/Bureau, 47
Park City's Historic Main Street, 43
Park City Silver Mine Adventure, 44
Park City Ski Area, 46
Park City Visitors Center and Museum, 43
Patio Drive-In, 115
Paunsagaunt Wildlife Museum, 129
Payson, 84
Peach Days, 17
Peery's Egyptian Theater, 9
Peppermint Place, 55
Perry, 14
Pickleville Playhouse, 24
Pineview Reservoir, 12
Pioneer Memorial Museum, 37
Pioneer Village, 4
Plymouth, 17
Pony Express Days (Clarkston), 25
Pony Express Trail, 62
Pow Wow and All-Indian Rodeo (Fort Duchesne), 88
Powder Mountain Ski Resort, 12

Pre-History Week (Price), 71
Price, 70
Price Canyon Recreation Area, 71
Price City Desert Wave Pool, 71
Promised Valley Playhouse, 34
Promontory, 15
Provo, 63
Provo Canyon, 65

Q
Queen's Garden Trail, 133

R
Railroader's Festival, 15
Rainbow Bridge National Monument, 120
Rainbow Point, 132
Randall L. Jones Theatre, 127
Raspberry Days (Garden City), 23
Recapture Lodge, 116
Red Butte Garden and Arboretum, 39
Red Canyon (Bryce Canyon), 129
Red Canyon Lodge (Vernal), 91
Red Canyon Overlook (Vernal), 95
Red Fleet Reservoir State Park, 95
Re-enactment of the Driving of the Golden Spike, 15
Reflections on the Ancients, 72, 75
Remains To Be Seen, 90
Rendezvous Beach (Bear Lake), 23
Rim Trail, 133
Rio Grande Cafe, 35
Rio Grande Railroad Depot, 35
Riverside Walk, 139
Roadside Ruin hike, 110
Rock Garden, 65
Rockreation Sport Climbing Center, 40
Rockville, 142
Rough Rider Days Rodeo (Roosevelt), 91

Roy, 7
Roy Historical Museum, 7
Raging Waters, 40
Royal Feaste, 127
Ruby's Inn, 130
Ruby's Inn Rodeo, 130

S
Salina, 80
Salt Lake Art Center, 34
Salt Lake Buzz, 34
Salt Lake City, 27
Salt Lake City Mormon Tabernacle, 30
Salt Palace Convention Center, 34
Salt Lake City Visitor Information Center, 34
Saltair, 49
San Juan County Travel Council, 114
San Juan River, 116, 117
San Rafael Swell, 74
San Rafael Trailrides, 75
Sand Island, 116, 117
Sandy, 42
Santaquin, 84
Scandinavian Festival (Ephraim), 83
Scenic Aviation (Blanding), 113
Scofield State Park, 72
Scottish Festival (Payson), 85
Seagull Monument, 29
Seven Peaks Water Park, 64
Sevier, 80
Shakespeare Festival (Cedar City), 125
Shaman Lodge, 71
Sheep Creek Geological Loop, 95
Sheri Griffith Expeditions, 103
Sherwood Hills Resort, 19
Sid's Mountain Wilderness Study Area, 75

Silver Pick, 92
Silver Putt Mini Golf, 45
Sink Hollow, 23
Skyline Drive, 1
Slickrock Trail, 103
Snow Canyon State Park, 144
Snowbasin Ski Resort, 12
Snowbird Ski Resort, 43
Soar Utah, 59
Solitude Nordic Center, 42
Solitude Ski Resort, 42
South Willow Canyon, 51
Spanish Fork, 68
Spanish Fork Community Water Park, 68
Speed Week (Bonneville Salt Flats), 54
Sports Park, 42
Split Mountain, 93
Spring City, 83
Spring Creek Park, 91
Spring Hollow, 21
Spring Salon (Springville), 67
Springdale, 138
Springville, 67
Springville Art Museum, 67
Springville World Folkfest, 67
Squaw Flats, 109
Squaw Peak Trail, 66
St. Christopher's Episcopal Mission, 116
St. George, 142
St. George Arts Festival, 143
St. George Mormon Temple, 143
Stage Stop Theatre, 25
Stagecoach Inn State Park, 62
Starvation Reservoir State Park, 88
State Fish Hatchery and Game Farm (Springville), 67
Steinaker Reservoir State Park, 95
Stewart Falls, 66

Strawberry Reservoir, 88
Summerfest (Bountiful), 3
Summerfest, (Logan), 19
Sunbonnet Cafe, 116
Sundance Children's Theater, 66
Sundance Resort, 66
Swasey's Cabin, 75
Swiss Days (Midway), 59
Syracuse, 5

T
Tag-A-Long Tours, 102
Temple of the Sun and Moon, 80
Temple Square (Salt Lake City), 29
Temple Square Visitor Centers, 30
Territorial Statehouse State Park, 82
Thanksgiving Point Botanical Gardens, 60
Thiokol Rocket Display, 15
This Is The Place State Park, 39
Thor's Hammer, 133
Timpanogos Cave National Monument, 57
Timpanogos Storytelling Festival (Orem), 62
Tintic Mining Museum, 84
Tintic National Historic Mining Area, 84
Tony Grove Lake, 22
Tooele, 51
Tooele Arts Festival, 52
Tooele Chamber of Commerce, 52
Tooele Railroad Museum, 51
Torrey, 77
Trafalga Fun Center, 63
Tree of Life, 53
Triad Center, 34
Tracy Aviary, 38
Trading Post, 101

Treehouse Children's Museum, 10
Tremonton, 17
Trolley Square, 37
Tuacahn, 144
Turtle Rock, 93
Twin Rocks Trading Post, 116

U
U-Bar Ranch, 91
Uinta Crest Fault, 95
Uintah-Ouray Indian Reservation, 88
Union Pacific Museum, Brigham City, 15
Union Station, 9
University of Utah, 38
Upheaval Dome Crater View Trail, 111
Utah Arts Festival, 34
Utah Botanical Gardens, 4
Utah Fun Dome, 41
Utah Jazz, 34
Utah Lake State Park, 64
Utah Mountain Llamas, 68
Utah Museum of Natural History (Salt Lake City), 38
Utah Navajo Fair Rodeo (Bluff), 116
Utah State Capitol, 36
Utah State Railroad Museum, 9
Utah State University, 20
Utah State University Discovery Center, 20
Utah State University Food Science Building, 20
Utah Valley Convention and Visitors Bureau, 63
Utah Valley Llama Fest (Spanish Fork), 68
Utah Waterfowl Management Area (Brown's Park), 98

Utah Winter Sports Park, 46
Ute Stampede Rodeo (Nephi), 83

V
Valle's Trading Post, 121
Valley of the Gods, 117
Valley View Riding Stables, 47
Vernal, 88
Virgin River, 139

W
Wahweap Marina, 120
Wasatch-Cache National Forest, 21
Wasatch Mountain State Park, 60
Washington Square, 35
Waterpocket Fold, 77
Wattis-Dumke Model Railroad Museum, 9
Weber State University, 9
Wedge Overlook, 74
Weeping Rock Trail, 139
Wellington, 72
Wellsville Mountains, 19
Wendover, 52
Wendover Air Base, 54
West Jordan, 48
Western Heritage Museum and Convention Center, 90
Western Mining and Railroad Museum (Helper), 69
Wheeler Historic Farm, 40
White Mesa Ute Council Bear Dance (Bluff), 116
White Pine Touring Center, 47
Wide Hollow Reservoir, 136
Wild Rivers Expeditions, 117
Willard, 13
Willard Bay State Park, 13
Willow Park, 20
Wilson Arch, 113
Wind Caves, 21
Windows, The, 106
Wolf Mountain, 46

Y
Ya Gotta Wanna Fun Park, 102

Z
ZCMI Center, 33
Zion Canyon Cinemax Theater, 141
Zion Factory Stores, 143
Zion Lodge, 140
Zion National Park, 138
Zion View Ranch, 145
Zion Visitor Center, 140

ACTIVITIES INDEX

FUN CENTERS
Alpine Slide, 45
Aquanoodle Slide, 91
Butch Cassidy Water Slide, 101
Cherry Hill Campground, 4
Classic Skating and Waterslides, 63
Dinah Bowl, 91
Fiesta Family Fun Center, 143
Fun City USA Water Slide Park, 9
Hogle Zoological Gardens, 40
Hydrosauras Slide, 91
Lagoon Amusement Park, 3
Lagoon-A-Beach, 4
Little Miner's Park, 45
Ogden Ice Sheet, 9
Paradise Pond, 57
Park City Silver Mine Adventure, 44
Pioneer Village, 4
Price City Desert Wave Pool, 71
Rock Garden, 65
Rockreation Sport Climbing Center, 40
Seven Peaks Water Park, 64
Silver Putt Mini Golf, 45
Spanish Fork Community Water Park, 68
Sports Park, 42
Spring Creek Park, 91
Trafalga Fun Center, 63
Utah Fun Dome, 41
Ya Gotta Wanna Fun Park, 102

PARKS
Anasazi Indian Village State Park, 137
Antelope Island State Park, 5
Arches National Park, 104
Bear Lake State Park, 23
Bryce Canyon National Park, 129, 130
Camp Floyd State Park, 61
Canyonlands National Park, 108
Capitol Reef National Park, 77
Cedar Breaks National Monument, 127
Coral Pink Sand Dunes State Park, 138
Dead Horse Point State Park, 112
Deer Creek Reservoir and State Park, 59
Dinosaur Gardens, 90
Dinosaur National Monument, 93
Eccles Dinosaur Park, 11
Edge of the Cedars State Park, 115
Escalante State Park, 136
Flaming Gorge National Recreation Area, 94
Field House of Natural History State Park, 88
Fort Buenaventura State Park, 8
Fremont Indian State Park, 80
Gallivan Utah Center, 35
Goblin Valley State Park, 76
Golden Spike National Historic Site, 15
Goosenecks of the San Juan State Park, 121
Great Salt Lake State Park, 49
Green River State Park, 75
Horseshoe Canyon, 112
Hovenweep National Monument, 117
Hyrum State Park, 18
International Peace Gardens, 40
Iron Mission State Park, 127
Island In The Sky, 111
Kodachrome Basin State Park, 135
Kolob Canyons, 145
Liberty Park, 37
Marble Park, 15
The Maze, 109
Memory Grove, 36
Mountain Bike Park, 129
The Needles, 109

Ogden River Parkway, 12
Old Deseret Village, 39
Rainbow Bridge National Monument, 120
Red Butte Garden and Arboretum, 39
Red Fleet Reservoir State Park, 95
Rendezvous Beach (Bear Lake), 23
Saltair, 49
Scofield State Park, 72
Snow Canyon State Park, 144
Spring Creek Park, 91
Stagecoach Inn State Park, 62
Starvation Reservoir State Park, 87
Steinaker Reservoir State Park, 95
This Is The Place State Park, 39
Timpanogos Cave National Monument, 57
Tracy Aviary, 38
Utah Botanical Gardens, 4
Utah Lake State Park, 64
Wasatch Mountain State Park, 60
Willard Bay State Park, 13
Willow Park, 19
Zion National Park, 138

ACCOMMODATIONS

Alta Ski Resort, 43
Beaver Creek Lodge, 23
Belmont Hot Springs Resort, 17
Brighton Ski Resort, 42
Bryce Canyon Lodge, 134
Bullfrog Marina, 118
Cherry Hill Campground, 4
Crystal Hot Springs Resort, 17
Deer Valley Resort, 46
Flaming Gorge Lodge, 96
Halls Crossing Marina, 118
Hite Marina, 120
Homestead Resort, 59
MD Ranchhouse, 114
Mountain Spaa Resort, 59
Park City Ski Area, 46
Pioneer Village Campground, 4
Powder Mountain Ski Resort, 12
Recapture Lodge, 117
Red Canyon Lodge, 91
Ruby's Inn, 130
Shaman Lodge, 71
Sherwood Hills Resort, 19
Snowbird Ski Resort, 43
Solitude Ski Resort, 42
Sundance Resort, 66
U-Bar Ranch, 91
Valle's Trading Post, 121
Wolf Mountain, 46
Zion Lodge, 140

CITIES AND REGIONS

Alpine, 55
American Fork, 57
Ashley National Forest, 95
Bear Lake, 23
Big Cottonwood Canyon, 42
Blanding, 114
Bluff, 115
Bluffdale, 47
Bonneville Salt Flats, 53
Boulder, 137
Bountiful, 1
Brian Head, 128
Brigham City, 15
Brown's Park, 96
Cannonville, 135
Castle Dale, 73
Cedar City, 125
Centerville, 3
Cleveland, 73
Colorado River, 102, 103, 118

ACTIVITIES INDEX

Copperton, 47
Cove Fort, 81
Duchesne, 87
Dutch John, 94
Eden, 13
Ephraim, 83
Escalante, 136
Eureka, 84
Fairfield, 61
Farmington, 3
Flaming Gorge National Recreation Area, 94
Fillmore, 82
Fort Duchesne, 87
Four Corners, 124
Fruit Heights, 4
Fruita, 78
Garden City, 23
Grafton, 142
Grantsville, 50
Great Salt Lake Desert, 52
Green River, 75, 96, 103
Green River City, 75
Halls Crossing, 118
Hanksville, 76
Heber, 58
Helper, 69
Hite Marina, 120
Honeyville, 17
Huntsville, 13
Hurricane, 144
Hyrum, 17
Jensen, 91
Kanab, 137
Kanarraville, 145
Kolob Canyons, 145
Lake Point, 48
Lake Powell, 118
LaSal Junction, 113

Layton, 5
Lehi, 60
Little Cottonwood Canyon, 42
Little Sahara Sand Dunes, 83
Logan, 18
Logan Canyon, 21
Manila, 94
Manti, 82
Mercur, 52
Mexican Hat, 121
Midway, 59
Mills Junction, 50
Moab, 99
Moki Dugway, 122
Monticello, 114
Monument Valley, 123
Murray, 41
Nephi, 83
Ogden, 7
Ogden Canyon, 12
Ophir, 52
Orem, 62
Panguitch, 129
Park City, 43
Payson, 84
Perry, 14
Plymouth, 17
Price, 70
Promontory, 15
Provo, 63
Rockville, 142
Roy, 7
Salina, 80
Salt Lake City, 27
San Juan River, 116, 117
San Rafael Swell, 74
Sandy, 42
Santaquin, 84
Sevier, 80

South Willow Canyon, 51
Spanish Fork, 68
Spring City, 83
Springdale, 138
Springville, 67
St. George, 142
Syracuse, 5
Tooele, 51
Torrey, 77
Tremonton, 17
Valley of the Gods, 117
Vernal, 88
Virgin River, 139
Wahweap Marina, 120
Wasatch-Cache National Forest, 21
Wellington, 72
Wellsville Mountains, 19
Wendover, 52
West Jordan, 48
Willard, 13

FESTIVALS AND RODEOS

America's Freedom Festival (Provo), 65
Art City Days (Springville), 67
Bear Dance (Fort Duchesne), 88
Belly Dance Festival, 38
Black and White Days (Richmond), 25
Black Diamond Stampede Rodeo (Price), 71
Cow Country Rodeo (Manila), 96
Dinosaur Days (Vernal), 91
Dinosaur Round-Up Rodeo (Vernal), 91
Electric Light Parade (Helper), 70
Fall Colors Fat Tire Bike Ride (Brian Head), 129
Fat Tire Festival (Moab), 103
Festival of Lights (Manila), 96
Festival of Lights (Spanish Fork), 68
Festival of the American West (Logan), 21
Festival of the Old West (Tooele), 52
Golden Onion Days (Payson), 85
Greek Festival Days (Price), 71
Greenshow, 127
Head Start Days (Bluff), 116
Heritage Days (Spring City), 83
Huck Finn Day (Provo), 65
Indian Day Celebration (Bluff), 116
International Folk Festival (Price), 71
International Peace Gardens, 40
Lehi Round-Up Rodeo, 61
Martin Harris Pageant (Clarkston), 25
Melon Days (Green River), 76
Mountain Man Rendezvous (Bear Lake), 23
Mormon Miracle Pageant, 82
Ogden Christmas Village, 10
Ogden-Hof Winter Carnival, 11
Ogden River Parkway Festival, 12
Oktoberfest (Brian Head), 129
Oktoberfest (Snowbird), 43
Outlaw Trail Festival (Vernal), 91
Pages Lane Theater, 3
Park City Arts Festival, 44
Peach Days (Brigham City), 17
Pony Express Days (Clarkston), 25
Pow Wow and All-Indian Rodeo (Fort Duchesne), 88
Pre-History Week (Price), 71
Railroader's Festival, 15
Raspberry Days (Garden City), 23
Rough Rider Days Rodeo (Roosevelt), 91
Royal Feaste, 127
Ruby's Inn Rodeo, 130
Scandinavian Festival (Ephraim), 83

ACTIVITIES INDEX

Scottish Festival (Payson), 85
Shakespeare Festival (Cedar City), 125
Speed Week (Bonneville Salt Flats), 54
Spring Salon (Springville), 67
Springville World Folkfest, 67
St. George Arts Festival, 143
Summerfest (Bountiful), 3
Summerfest (Logan), 19
Swiss Days (Midway), 59

Timpanogos Storytelling Festival (Orem), 62
Tooele Arts Festival, 52
Utah Arts Festival, 34
Utah Navajo Fair Rodeo (Bluff), 116
Utah Valley Llama Fest (Spanish Fork), 68
Ute Stampede Rodeo (Nephi), 83
White Mesa Ute Council Bear Dance (Bluff), 116

ABOUT THE AUTHOR

Margaret Sandberg Godfrey is a life-long resident of Utah. She spends most of her free time exploring Utah with her family in searching for adventures. She works as special project coordinator for the Utah State Travel Development office and has written dozens of travel articles for local and national magazines. She is a freelance writer and a regular contributor to the *Salt Lake Tribune* and *Enterprise* newspapers.

Also of Interest from The Globe Pequot Press

Off The Beaten Path: Texas $12.95
Features lesser-known sites of interest that resonate with local color and touch the true heart of the region.

Day Trips From Houston $12.95
Getaways less than two hours away.

Quick Escapes from Dallas/Fort Worth $13.95
35 weekend getaways in and around the Lone Star State.

Woodall's Camping Guide: Frontier West $5.99
Complete guide to campgrounds and attractions in Texas, Arkansas, Mexico, Oklahoma, Kansas, and New Mexico.

50 Great Family Vacations: Western North America $18.95
Great things for the entire family to see and do in the Western States.

Other titles in this series:
The Family Adventure Guides™ are available for almost every state in the country.

Available from your bookstore or directly from the publisher. For a catalogue or to place an order, call toll-free 24 hours a day (1-800-243-0495), or write to The Globe Pequot Press, P.O. Box 833, Old Saybrook, Connecticut 06475-0833.